I0800646

STUDY GUIDE

Created for Worship

Jason Helopoulos

LIGONIER MINISTRIES
Renew your Mind.
LIGONIER.ORG | 800-435-4343

421 Ligonier Court, Sanford, FL 32771
Email: info@ligonier.org

Printed in China.

Contents

Introduction

One of the most fundamental questions that we can ask is "Why are we here?" God created us with a purpose—to worship Him. In *Created for Worship,* Jason Helopoulos helps us to refocus on our true calling as worshipers. In Christ, we have been re-created to worship God in spirit and truth, and part of what this means is knowing what worship is all about. Worship is what we were created for and worship is what we are destined for, that we will one day worship God in His presence for all eternity.

This study guide is a companion to the video teaching series. Whether you are using the DVDs, streaming the videos on Ligonier.org, or going through the course in Ligonier Connect, this resource is designed to help you make the most of the learning experience. For each message in the series, there is a corresponding lesson in this guide. Here is what you will find in each lesson:

INTRODUCTION	The introduction is a brief paragraph that summarizes the content covered in the lecture and considered in the study guide lesson. **How to use:** Use the introduction to each lesson to get a sense of the big picture before watching the video. Refer to these statements as you work through the study guide to remind yourself of what you have already covered and where you are headed.
LEARNING GOALS	The learning goals are the knowledge and skills the study guide lesson will endeavor to equip you with as you work through the lecture content. **How to use:** Familiarize yourself with the goals of each lesson before engaging with its contents. Keeping the overall purpose in mind as you watch each video and reflect on or discuss the questions will help you get the most out of each lesson.
KEY IDEAS	The key ideas are the major points or takeaways from the lecture. **How to use:** Use these ideas to prepare yourself for each lesson and to review previous lessons. They describe specifically the knowledge each lecture is communicating.

REFLECTION & DISCUSSION QUESTIONS	The questions are the guided reflection and/or discussion component of the lesson that are intended to help you prepare for, process, and organize what you are learning. **How to use:** Reflect on individually or discuss in a group the questions in the order in which they appear in the lesson. The time stamps in the right margin indicate where the answers to questions during the video can be found.
PRAYER	The prayer section offers suggestions for how to close the lesson in prayer with respect to what was taught in the lecture. **How to use:** Consider using each lesson's prayer section as a guide to personal or group prayer. These sections follow the ACTS prayer model, which you can learn more about in R.C. Sproul's Crucial Questions booklet *Does Prayer Change Things?* This helpful guide is available as a free e-book at Ligonier.org.
REVIEW QUIZ	The review quiz is a set of six multiple-choice questions that appears at the end of each lesson. **How to use:** Use each quiz to check your comprehension and memory of the major points covered in each lecture. It will be most beneficial to your learning if you take a lesson's quiz either sometime between lessons or just before you begin the next lesson in the study guide.
ANSWER KEY	The answer key provides explanations for the reflection and discussion questions and answers to the multiple-choice questions in the review quiz. **How to use:** Use the answer key to check your own answers or when you do not know the answer. Note: Do not give in too quickly; struggling for a few moments to recall an answer reinforces it in your mind.

Study Schedules

The following table suggests four plans for working through the *Created for Worship* video teaching series and this companion study guide. Whether you are going through this series on your own or with a group, these schedules should help you plan your study path.

	Extended 13-Week Plan	Standard 11-Week Plan	Abbreviated 5-Week Plan	Intensive 3-Week Plan
Week	**Lesson**			
1	*	1	1 & 2	1–4
2	1	2	3 & 4	5–8
3	2	3	5–7	9–11
4	3	4	8 & 9	
5	4	5	10 & 11	
6	5	6		
7	6	7		
8	7	8		
9	8	9		
10	9	10		
11	10	11		
12	11			
13	*			

* For these weeks, rather than completing lessons, spend your time discussing and praying about your learning goals for the study (the first week) and the most valuable takeaways from the study (the last week).

1

Created to Be Worshipers

INTRODUCTION

As we consider God's work in creation, we learn about Him and see the reality of His majesty and the complexity of His nature. In light of this grandeur, we can feel small, frail, and inept. We wonder why God created us. In this lesson, Rev. Helopoulos discusses how Scripture reveals that God created men and women in His own image and gave them the purpose of reflecting His own image and filling creation with His glory.

LEARNING GOALS

When you have finished this lesson, you should be able to:

- Describe how the magnitude of creation reflects the greatness of God
- Identify main purposes for God's creation of humankind

KEY IDEAS

- Experiencing the wonder of the natural world leads us to consider the nature of God, the Creator, and the nature of humankind, the created.
- In the creation account, we see that God created men and women with the distinction of being made in His own image.
- Bearing God's image endows each human life with dignity and purpose: to bring honor and glory to God and to fill the earth as reflections of His image.

REFLECTION & DISCUSSION QUESTIONS

Before the Video

What Do You Think?

Take a moment to answer the following questions. They will prepare you for the lecture.

- Can you recall a time when you were awestruck by something you observed in creation? What did you see, and what did it cause you to think and feel?

- Why does humankind exist? Why did God choose to create us?

Scripture Reading

So God created man in his own image, in the image of God he created him; male and female he created them. And God blessed them. And God said to them, "Be fruitful and multiply and fill the earth and subdue it, and have dominion over the fish of the sea and over the birds of the heavens and over every living thing that moves on the earth."

—Genesis 1:27–28

- What commission did God give to the first man and woman, and how does His instruction to them reflect the fact that they bear His image?

During the Video

Answer the following questions while you watch the video. They will guide you through the lecture.

Why Are We Here? *0:00–9:15*

- In Psalm 8, what motivates David to worship the Lord?

- What are two primary ways in which God reveals Himself to us?

God's Purpose in Creating Humankind *9:15–22:21*

- Did God create humans because He needed them? Because He was lonely? Because He was bored? Why or why not?

- In Psalm 29, how does David's call for the angels to glorify God relate to us?

After the Video

Answer the following questions after you have finished the lecture. They will help you identify and summarize the major points.

- What does God reveal to us about Himself through the name that He made known to Moses in Exodus?

  If you are in a group, discuss how rightly reflecting on God's being and attributes can shape the Christian life. Ask: How can reflecting on attributes of God help you overcome times of difficulty?

- What are various reasons that people may struggle with the question "Why am I still here?" What do we need to bring to mind to recall our purpose or to minister to others?

  If you are in a group, discuss with the other members times when you have personally asked or have encountered someone else who was asking, "Why am I still here?" Ask: How would you present the gospel with reference to worship to someone struggling with this question?

- What is a time when you witnessed something in nature that drew you to worship God and glorify His name?

  If you are in a group, have the members share their experiences in the answers from the question above and read Psalm 8. Ask: Where else does Psalm 8 call us to experience God?

PRAYER

Commit what you have learned from God's Word in this lesson to prayer.

- Praise God for creating you in His image and revealing Himself to you through His creation.
- Confess the areas in which you are not living to reflect God's image for His glory and honor.
- Thank God for giving you life and breath to exist for His glory.
- Ask God to increase your awareness of His majesty, to give you eyes to see His good work in creation, and to grow your capacity for worshiping Him and delighting in Him.

REVIEW QUIZ

Use these multiple-choice questions to measure what you learned from this lesson.

1. Unlike the world and everything in it, there has never been a time a when God did not exist.
   a. True
   b. False

2. "O LORD, our Lord, how majestic is your name in all the earth!" is a quote from which of the following psalms?
   a. Psalm 139
   b. Psalm 29
   c. Psalm 19
   d. Psalm 8

3. In Genesis 1, we learn that only men were created in God's image.
   a. True
   b. False

4. Why did God call humans to be fruitful and multiply?
   a. To give them something to do
   b. To test them and measure their obedience
   c. To see His own image reflected in creation
   d. To punish them for the sin of eating of the tree

5. When God called Moses to deliver His people from bondage in Egypt, what name did He tell Moses to give when they ask, "What is his name?" (Ex. 3:13)?
   a. "The Lord God Almighty"
   b. "I AM WHO I AM"
   c. "The Creator God"
   d. "Deliverer"

6. What was the point of Jonathan Edwards' treatise *The End for Which God Created the World*?
   a. There is no meaning in the world greater than what we provide.
   b. All things were created to provide companionship for God.
   c. Creation will ultimately be restored.
   d. Everything exists for God's glory.

Answer Key—Created to Be Worshipers

REFLECTION & DISCUSSION QUESTIONS

Before the Video

What Do You Think?

These are personal questions. The answers should be based on your own knowledge and experience.

Scripture Reading

- What commission did God give to the first man and woman, and how does His instruction to them reflect the fact that they bear His image?

  God called Adam and Eve to be fruitful, to multiply, to fill the earth, to subdue it, and to have dominion over the other living things. God's likeness is reflected in the ability of humankind to invest in relationships, to nurture life and livelihoods, to oversee the flourishing of other living things, and to govern them—in essence, to serve as subcreators within God's created world.

During the Video

Why Are We Here?

- In Psalm 8, what motivates David to worship the Lord?

  David's observations about God's creation, greatness, and care for him and for all humankind lead him to worship. Creation reflects truth about the Creator and also about how we should respond to Him.

- What are two primary ways in which God reveals Himself to us?

  God reveals Himself to us by His works and by His names. God's works show us His power, His character, His presence, and His involvement in our world. The names by which God introduces Himself help us understand His nature and how we can relate to Him.

God's Purpose in Creating Humankind

- Did God create humans because He needed them? Because He was lonely? Because He was bored? Why or why not?

  No. God's fullness and sufficiency led Him to create out of His abundance so that the expression of His glory would be multiplied and lead to greater and greater honor and praise for His perfections.

- In Psalm 29, how does David's call for the angels to glorify God relate to us?

One type of creature alone cannot adequately reflect the fullness of God's glory or give Him sufficient praise. Therefore, all created things—including humankind—are meant to bring praise and glory to God and thus reflect and magnify the varied aspects of His glory.

After the Video

- What does God reveal to us about Himself through the name that He made known to Moses in Exodus?

  God reveals His name to Moses in Exodus 3:14: "God said to Moses, 'I AM WHO I AM.'" This is a name unlike any other. In this name, God communicates to us that He is pure being. He does not become or undergo change. He always is. He has always existed and has the power of existence in Himself. He is also ever only Himself. He is simple and not dependent on anything for His existence.

- What are various reasons that people may struggle with the question "Why am I still here?" What do we need to bring to mind to recall our purpose or to minister to others?

  The difficulties and pain of life can bring people to a point of wondering whether their lives have meaning and whether it's all worth it. Some of the examples that were given in this lecture of this was an elderly man whose body was failing him and a teenager struggling with peer pressure. Everyone is created to be worshipers, and we ought to worship God and praise Him wherever we find ourselves—even in the midst of the complexity of illness, pain, or other hardships. It is important to remember that if God has given us breath, there is a purpose for our living right now: worship.

- What is a time when you witnessed something in nature that drew you to worship God and glorify His name?

  The answers to this question are personal in nature but should reflect on the reality that God's creation reveals His existence and aspects of His nature. Wherever we live, in whatever season we find ourselves, we can encounter the wonder of God's created world and consider how it reflects His desire to fill the earth with His glory.

REVIEW QUIZ

1. **A.**
   There has never been a time when God has not existed. By His very nature, God exists. As Rev. Helopoulos stated: "He just is. He has always been and He always is and He always will be. . . . Everything else came to be. He just is."

2. **D.**
   "O LORD, our Lord, how majestic is your name in all the earth!" is a quotation from Psalm 8:1. We can imagine David's looking at God's creation in awe, marveling at His majesty as it is being reflected in the created order.

3. **B.**

   Both men and women are made in God's image. Genesis 1:27 records that "God created man in his own image, in the image of God he created him; male and female he created them."

4. **C.**

   In creation, humankind is the high point—not merely because of the wisdom or skill or beauty of humankind, but because men and women alone were created in God's image. God called them to multiply and to fill the earth with sons and daughters made in His image so that He might see Himself reflected in His creation.

5. **B.**

   Exodus 3:14: "God said to Moses, 'I AM WHO I AM.' And he said, 'Say this to the people of Israel: "I AM has sent me to you."'" God was communicating to Moses by this name His eternality, that He was, is, and always will be the one true and living God who has never come into being and never has been anything other than Himself.

6. **D.**

   Jonathan Edwards wrote the moving treatise The End for Which God Created the World *to articulate the point that everything exists for God's glory. God alone is worthy, having all glory in Himself, to have ordered all that He has created unto His glory.*

2

Re-Created for Worship

INTRODUCTION

After creation, it wasn't long before Adam and Eve faced the temptation to question God and to disobey His commands. They fell into sin. When God responded with judgment, He also foretold of redemption to come through the woman's offspring. God ordained a way to restore His purpose to fill the earth with His image and His worshipers. For the Christian, all of life is now about living as a re-created worshiper for God's glory.

LEARNING GOALS

When you have finished this lesson, you should be able to:

- Explain how God's response to the fall brought not only punishment for sin but also a promise for redemption
- Describe the "pilgrim" concept of living as a traveler from this world to the next and understand how this way of life is fueled by worship and a desire to see more and more of the beauty of Christ

KEY IDEAS

- When Adam and Eve rebelled against God, the human race marred God's image and purpose in creation to fill the world with His glory.
- By God's merciful kindness and almighty power, the promised redemption through Christ provides a way for people to be restored as image bearers and re-created as worshipers for the glory of God.
- The Great Commission reflects the creation mandate: followers of Jesus are to make disciples of all nations and thus fill the earth with worshipers of Christ and reflections of God's glory.

REFLECTION & DISCUSSION QUESTIONS

Before the Video

What Do You Think?

Take a moment to answer the following questions. They will prepare you for the lecture.

- How does the fall of Adam and Eve into sin affect your life today? Because they fell into sin, what must happen for God's purpose for humankind to be worshipers to be fulfilled?

- What have you observed about the way in which the Bible presents worship? Can you think of passages that give instruction on the practice of worship, examples of worship, or descriptions of what worship is?

Scripture Reading

I appeal to you therefore, brothers, by the mercies of God, to present your bodies as a living sacrifice, holy and acceptable to God, which is your spiritual worship. Do not be conformed to this world, but be transformed by the renewal of your mind, that by testing you may discern what is the will of God, what is good and acceptable and perfect.

—Romans 12:1–2

- The Apostle Paul calls us to lead lives of "spiritual worship" through the offering of our lives to God. In this call, what roles do the "mercies of God" and the "will of God" play?

During the Video

Answer the following questions while you watch the video. They will guide you through the lecture.

The Effect of the Fall on Our Calling as Worshipers *0:00–9:18*

- What happened to as a result of Adam's first transgression?

- How did John Calvin describe the human heart?

Re-Created: Living All of Life in Worship *9:18–22:21*

- What connects "duty" with "delight" in the Christian life?

- How does our sense of pilgrimage grow? How does this heighten our desires for obedience, praise, and enjoyment of God?

After the Video

Answer the following questions after you have finished the lecture. They will help you identify and summarize the major points.

- In what manner did Satan tempt Eve? By recognizing Satan's temptation tactics with Eve, can you trace similar paths of temptation in your own life?

  If you are in a group, discuss observations about Eve's temptation and share any parallels to your own experience or to patterns you have observed in human nature. Ask: How do these experiences shed light on what people believe about God and about His care for them?

- Does God's response to Adam and Eve's sin surprise you in any way? Why or why not?

  If you are in a group, invite the members to share times when they have observed or received God's mercy through Christ following a sinful act. Ask: How does that mercy affect how you think and feel about your sin and about God?

- How does the "pilgrim" concept give you hope? Are you engaged in things that are entangling you in this present world? If so, what must be done?

  If you are in a group, discuss the dangers of forgetting that we are pilgrims in this world.

PRAYER

Commit what you have learned from God's Word in this lesson to prayer.

- Praise God for His merciful provision of a Redeemer to restore you from a life of sin and death.
- Confess to God any areas of doubting His goodness or rebellion against His commands, and ask for His forgiveness through Christ.

- Thank God for the gift of Christ and for the salvation that allows you to worship Him and to live for His glory.
- Ask God to help you to walk in His ways, following Christ in all that you say and do, that your life might reflect the glory of God and bring honor to Him.

REVIEW QUIZ

Use these multiple-choice questions to measure what you learned from this lesson.

1. After the creation of Adam and Eve, which of the following did *not* happen?
   a. Adam and Eve enjoyed God's presence in the garden.
   b. Adam and Eve resisted the temptation to eat the forbidden fruit.
   c. God found Adam and Eve and confronted them with their sin.
   d. God proclaimed the punishment of Adam and Eve along with a merciful promise.

2. In what way has the "cosmic rebellion" against God *not* affected all humankind?
   a. We are now all born in sin.
   b. Each person has a fallen mind and a fallen heart.
   c. We are in complete and utter rebellion against God.
   d. We have a desire to worship God, just not the ability.

3. When the Apostle Paul wrote to the Ephesians, what purpose did he name for the adoption of believers through Christ?
   a. To bless us "with every spiritual blessing in Christ"
   b. "That we should be holy and blameless before him"
   c. That we should be "to the praise of his glorious grace"
   d. That we would "present [our] bodies as a living sacrifice"

4. In *Let the Nations Be Glad,* John Piper wrote that missions exist because joy doesn't.
   a. True
   b. False

5. The mandate in the garden to "be fruitful and multiply" (Gen. 1:28) is now reflected in the Great Commission of Jesus to "go therefore and make disciples of all nations" (Matt. 28:19).
   a. True
   b. False

6. To live as a "pilgrim" implies which mentality?
   a. We are going from here to there.
   b. This life does not truly matter in light of eternity.
   c. Our choices are inconsequential.
   d. We are meant to live for now.

Answer Key—Re-Created for Worship

REFLECTION & DISCUSSION QUESTIONS

Before the Video

What Do You Think?

These are personal questions. The answers should be based on your own knowledge and experience.

Scripture Reading

- The Apostle Paul calls us to lead lives of "spiritual worship" through the offering of our lives to God. In this call, what roles do the "mercies of God" and the "will of God" play?

  The mercies of God make a way for redemption from rebellion against God, that followers of Christ would seek after the will of God—what is good, acceptable, and perfect. If time allows, discover more of the context of Paul's often-quoted appeal in Romans 12:1–2 by reading Romans 11. Begin reading at verse 25 or earlier to gain perspective on God's mercy in bringing about our redemption.

During the Video

The Effect of the Fall on Our Calling as Worshipers

- What happened to us as a result of Adam's first transgression?

  The Westminster Shorter Catechism affirms that "all mankind, descending from him by ordinary generation, sinned in him, and fell with him, in his first transgression" (WSC 16). The state of sin that we have fallen into is described excellently in the next answer of the catechism: "The sinfulness of that estate whereinto man fell, consists in the guilt of Adam's first sin, the want of original righteousness, and the corruption of his whole nature, which is commonly called Original Sin; together with all actual transgressions which proceed from it" (WSC 18).

- How did John Calvin describe the human heart?

  Calvin described the fallen human heart as an idol factory. In our lives, we continually shape and mold idols of our own making to worship and to center our lives upon, to direct our minds and our affections towards.

Re-Created: Living All of Life in Worship

- What connects "duty" with "delight" in the Christian life?

  Encountering Christ changes a person's life. Someone might react negatively to the idea that it is our duty to worship, but when we have a relationship with

Christ, worship is also a delight. In the Westminster Shorter Catechism, the answer to the first question proclaims that the chief end of man is to glorify God and to enjoy Him forever. God in His exceeding kindness has created us so that His purpose for our lives to be worshipers is also what will bring us the most delight.

- How does our sense of pilgrimage grow? How does this heighten our desires for obedience, praise, and enjoyment of God?

  The more we see of the beauty of Christ, the more we long to see more of it. When we see and appreciate more and more of the beauty of Christ, we long more and more to hear His Word, to speak to Him in prayer, to love His people, to sing His praise, and to be prepared to be with Him in glory for eternity.

After the Video

- In what manner did Satan tempt Eve? By recognizing Satan's temptation tactics with Eve, can you trace similar paths of temptation in your own life?

  He drew Eve's attention away from God's presence and provision for her and introduced questions about God's care and intentions in keeping the forbidden fruit from her. Since that day, these patterns of temptation have been thread through the lives of every man and woman. When we begin to question God's presence, power, provision, and purpose, we can be led to believe any number of lies about God, about ourselves, and about our world. This deception leads us to abandon God's presence and His commands and to forge ahead in our own rebellious way. When you have fallen into sin, try to identify the question that the temptation posed about God and your relationship to Him and the lie that you believed that led you to sin.

- Does God's response to Adam and Eve's sin surprise you in any way? Why or why not?

  Following their sin, Adam and Eve did not seek out God's presence to confess and ask forgiveness. They hid from Him. Even when God found them and they spoke to Him about their sin, they tried to hide by blaming others. Although Adam and Eve did not comprehend the scope of their sin—neither the magnitude of their offense against their Creator nor the far-reaching results of their actions—God did not obliterate them in wrath as He could have done. Nor did God ignore or excuse the sin. God came to Adam and Eve and engaged them about the sin. He brought it into the light and addressed what had taken place. God disbursed judgment that was fitting and yet merciful.

- How does the "pilgrim" concept give you hope? Are you engaged in things that are entangling you in this present world? If so, what must be done?

  Looking toward our heavenly home with Christ can help give realistic perspective to the temptations we face and the challenges we endure. Knowing that glory awaits will motivate us to follow Christ, to bear our cross, and to keep our eyes on the promises of God.

REVIEW QUIZ

1. **B.**
   Adam and Eve did not resist the temptation of the serpent. In Genesis 3:6, we read that Eve "took of its fruit and ate, and she also gave some to her husband who was with her, and he ate."

2. **D.**
   The fall has affected our whole natures in a radical way. Both the way we think and the way we act are affected by sin. Even our desires are fallen. In complete rebellion against God, we do not want to worship Him and are in need of His grace.

3. **C.**
   "In love he predestined us for adoption to himself as sons through Jesus Christ, according to the purpose of his will, to the praise of his glorious grace, *with which he has blessed us in the Beloved" (Eph. 1:4–6).*

4. **B.**
   John Piper wrote, "Missions exist because worship doesn't." This drives home the priority of the worship of God in our lives, the reason that we are saved, and the reason that we go on missions: that others also might be saved unto worship.

5. **A.**
   As God first commanded Adam and Eve to fill the earth and subdue it, now followers of Jesus are to go out to make disciples of Christ and to spread His teaching so that where God's image has been marred by sin, it can be restored to once again reflect the glory of God. Thus, God's original purpose in the creation mandate to fill the earth with His image and glory can be fulfilled through Christ's saving work, reaching all nations and drawing men and women from every tribe and tongue to live as re-created worshipers of God.

6. **A.**
   To live as a pilgrim means that one is "going from here to there." A pilgrim lives as one on a journey toward a destination, toward a settled dwelling. Each of a pilgrim's decisions will either help or hinder the journey, making the way simple, steady, and direct or inviting complications, delays, and detours. A pilgrim lives in hope for reaching a final goal and destination.

3

Word-Centered Worship

INTRODUCTION

For the Christian, corporate worship is the high point of life. Each week, God meets with His people, and His people meet with Him. Jesus taught that God is seeking worshipers and that worship is to be done in spirit and truth. Therefore, we look to God to renew our spirits by the Holy Spirit so that we are engaged in worship, and we fill worship with the Word of God so that our worship is centered on the truth.

LEARNING GOALS

When you have finished this lesson, you should be able to:

- Understand what God desires of our worship
- Discuss the essence of worship as a state of being
- Identify the characteristics of true worship that Jesus spoke of in John 4
- Describe the regulatory principle and the elements, forms, and circumstances of worship

KEY IDEAS

- In worship, God meets with us, and we meet with God. Therefore, worship is never casual or boring.
- Corporate worship should not be defined by what we imagine that we should do in worship or by what we think others would be drawn to in worship.
- Corporate worship is to be defined by what God has revealed about worship—that it is to be done in simplicity and sincerity, in spirit and in truth.

REFLECTION & DISCUSSION QUESTIONS

Before the Video

What Do You Think?

Take a moment to answer the following questions. They will prepare you for the lecture.

- Scripture teaches that God is omnipresent and always with us, so why are worship services needed? What happens in corporate worship?
- How should the nature of God and His relationship with His children shape the structure and experience of corporate worship?

Scripture Reading

How lovely is your dwelling place, O Lord *of hosts! My soul longs, yes, faints for the courts of the* Lord*; my heart and flesh sing for joy to the living God.*

—Psalm 84:1–2

- As the psalmist considers gathering for worship, what is he focused on? What emotions does he express?

During the Video

Answer the following questions while you watch the video. They will guide you through the lecture.

The Essence of Worship — *0:00–14:30*

- How do the Ten Commandments relate to corporate worship?
- What's wrong with the idea that worship is "casual"?

The Manner of Worship — *14:30–24:04*

- What is an alternative to seeker-sensitive worship? What did Jesus reveal about the manner of true worship?

- What is an example in the Old Testament of how seriously God takes worship?

After the Video

Answer the following questions after you have finished the lecture. They will help you identify and summarize the major points.

- What was the Reformation about? Taken together with what happens in corporate worship as described in this lesson, does this change how you have perhaps thought about worship? Why or why not?

  If you are in a group, invite the members to discuss their experiences in worship. Ask: Is the idea of meeting with God regularly in mind? If so, how does that concept influence engagement in worship? If not, how would that concept change the experience of worship?

- What does it mean that true worship is "in spirit and truth"?

  If you are in a group, discuss how "spirit" and "truth" together create a unique experience in worship. Ask: How can you tell whether one is missing? What have you encountered in worship services that helps or hinders engaging in spirit and truth?

- What are the "elements" and "forms" of worship? Are the forms or circumstances of worship matters of indifference? Why or why not?

  If you are in a group, ask whether group members have attended worship services when traveling away from home, perhaps in other churches or in other countries. Discuss similarities and differences between these worship experiences.

PRAYER

Commit what you have learned from God's Word in this lesson to prayer.

- Praise God for His presence with you and His invitation to meet with Him in corporate worship each week.
- Confess to God any disinterest in corporate worship or reluctance to gather, and ask God for His cleansing and rejuvenating of your desire to meet with Him and His people corporately.
- Thank God for the community of the local believers with whom you worship and the many varied members of the body of Christ.

- Ask God to renew your spirit for worship each week, that you would be engaged with reading, hearing, and learning from His Word.

REVIEW QUIZ

Use these multiple-choice questions to measure what you learned from this lesson.

1. Our study will unpack three spheres of worship. Which of the following does *not* belong?
   a. Corporate worship
   b. Family worship
   c. Secret worship
   d. Service-oriented worship

2. When we meet with God, it must be in spirit and truth.
   a. True
   b. False

3. When John Calvin wrote to Charles V, which two things did he name as conveying the whole substance of Christianity?
   a. An understanding of worship (1) in spirit and (2) in truth
   b. Experience of (1) salvation in Christ and (2) witnessing to unbelievers
   c. Practice of (1) corporate worship and (2) family worship
   d. Knowledge of (1) the mode in which God is duly worshiped and (2) the source of salvation

4. In Psalm 42, the psalmist is referencing which sphere of worship when he writes, "As a deer pants for flowing streams, so pants my soul for you, O God"?
   a. Family worship
   b. Secret worship
   c. Corporate worship
   d. All of the above

5. How we worship when we gather is of minor importance to God.
   a. True
   b. False

6. Practicing the sacraments of baptism and the Lord's Supper falls into which category in our worship gatherings?
   a. Circumstances
   b. Forms
   c. Elements
   d. Spirit

Answer Key—Word-Centered Worship

REFLECTION & DISCUSSION QUESTIONS

Before the Video

What Do You Think?

These are personal questions. The answers should be based on your own knowledge and experience.

Scripture Reading

- As the psalmist considers gathering for worship, what is he focused on? What emotions does he express?

  The psalmist eagerly anticipates God's presence—he wants to see God's "dwelling place" and be in "the courts of the LORD." He is eager to express joy with his "heart and flesh" in song to "the living God." He is focused on experiencing God's presence in a specific place at a specific time. He will respond to that presence with worship and praise with his voice. The psalmist feels adoration, longing, anticipation, and joy. He awaits a sense of satisfaction in God's presence through praise.

During the Video

The Essence of Worship

- How do the Ten Commandments relate to corporate worship?

  The Ten Commandments were given to God's people after they were delivered from the bondage of slavery in Egypt. Now Israel's identity would be shaped by the nation's relationship with God and worship of God. In Exodus 20:2, God introduces the Ten Commandments by saying, "I am the LORD your God, who brought you out of the land of Egypt, out of the house of slavery." God's own identity and His relationship to the people provide the framework for the following commands about relating to God and about relating to one another. The first four commandments specifically describe how the people are to relate to God Himself in worship.

- What's wrong with the idea that worship is "casual"?

  In the current culture of the United States, "casual" worship is often praised because it is informal in tone and setting and thus thought to be more accessible for those who are curious about the Christian faith. Although God gives a ready welcome to those who come to Him through Christ, He does not present Himself as casually approachable in Scripture. God is significantly "other" than us. He is holy. When we lose sight of this reality, our worship loses substance and meaning.

We are to engage in worship that truthfully reflects our relationship with God and His with us.

The Manner of Worship

- What is an alternative to seeker-sensitive worship? What did Jesus reveal about the manner of true worship?

  God also has something to say about how *we worship Him. Worship is not to be fashioned after popular trends or what we think people want. Worship is to be centered on God—"God-sensitive worship," if you will. Jesus revealed to the woman at the well exactly what this means: we must worship God "in spirit and truth" (John 4:24).*

- What is an example in the Old Testament of how seriously God takes worship?

  Scripture shows that how we worship God matters to God. Much of the Bible is devoted to describing worship practices and worship spaces, especially in the old covenant with the tabernacle, the temple, and the sacrificial system. The example of Nadab and Abihu in Leviticus 10 is a case in point. These men were struck dead because of unauthorized worship practices, offering "strange fire" to the Lord. Not being authorized from God, this worship was not in accord with truth.

After the Video

- What was the Reformation about? Taken together with what happens in corporate worship as described in this lesson, does this change how you have perhaps thought about worship? Why or why not?

  While the Reformation was certainly about the authority of Scripture and the essence of justification, it can be argued that the Reformation was also a liturgical renewal. The first element of what John Calvin called "the whole substance of Christianity" is knowing how God desires to be worshiped. This is because worship is fundamentally God's meeting with us and our meeting with God. It isn't a casual experience. Imagine meeting someone whose accomplishments you admire, whose counsel you long to hear, or whose character you respect. Meeting with a dynamic individual like that would not be an encounter you would take lightly. How much more so our encounter with the living, almighty, omnipotent, and eternal God.

- What does it mean that true worship is "in spirit and truth"?

  The woman of Samaria believed that worship was simply about being in the right place at the right time, doing the right thing. But God is not wanting us to merely check a box. Worship is about the heart. But to do this, we need God's help to worship truly through the renewal of the Holy Spirit. The Spirit engages our spirits in accordance with the truth of the Word of God, which tells us how to rightly worship Him.

- What are the "elements" and "forms" of worship? Are the forms or circumstances of worship matters of indifference? Why or why not?

  The forms and circumstances of worship vary from one place to another and from one time to another. While worship may look differently from one century to another or in different places around the globe, it will not be completely different because the elements of worship that God has revealed preserves the essence of worship. These elements were summarized by phrases all centering on God's Word: we read the Word, preach the Word, pray the Word, sing the Word, confess the Word, and see the Word in worship. Forms of worship, such as whether a prayer is extemporaneous or written, are not matters of total indifference; they must not do injustice to the elements of worship but rather serve to accentuate the elements of worship. Circumstances of worship, such as when then church meets on a Sunday morning, have been referred to as adiaphora, *matters of indifference.*

REVIEW QUIZ

1. **D.**
   The three spheres of worship are corporate worship, family worship, and secret (or private) worship. The concept of serving others as a form of worship, which could perhaps be included as a category of worship in all of life, was not identified as a sphere of worship to be explored.

2. **A.**
   Jesus said, "God is spirit, and those who worship him must worship in spirit and truth" (John 4:24). We must be truly engaged with God by the Holy Spirit, and we must worship God according to how He has told us to worship Him.

3. **D.**
   John Calvin wrote, "If it be inquired, then, by what things chiefly, the Christian religion has a standing existence among us, and maintains its truth, it will be found that the following two not only occupy the principal place, but comprehend under them all other parts, and consequently the whole substance of Christianity, viz., a knowledge first, of the mode in which God is duly worshiped; and secondly, of the source from which salvation is to be obtained."

4. **C.**
   In Psalm 42:2–4, the psalmist is calling to mind corporate worship settings: "When shall I come and appear before God? . . . These things I remember, as I pour out my soul: how I would go with the throng and lead them in procession to the house of God with glad shouts and songs of praise, a multitude keeping festival."

5. **B.**
   The call to worship in spirit and truth alone drives home the point that God takes worship seriously. Rev. Helopoulos stated, "How we worship when we gather is of extreme importance to God."

6. **C.**
The elements of worship include what God has told us should be present in worship: reading the Word, preaching the Word, praying the Word, singing the Word, confessing the Word, and seeing the Word of God played out in the practice of the sacraments of baptism and the Lord's Supper.

4

Created for Corporate Worship

INTRODUCTION

For the Christian, the practice of gathering with God's people weekly to meet and to worship Him is a priority. In Scripture, we find many analogies to help us understand the corporate nature of our faith: a flock, a building, a bride. In this lesson, Rev. Helopoulos discusses why gathering matters, how we can engage children in worship to shape the next generation, and how we can prepare to faithfully engage in worship and to treasure the Lord's Day.

LEARNING GOALS

When you have finished this lesson, you should be able to:

- Identify eight principles that should mark Christian corporate worship
- Discuss the analogies that God uses to describe the corporate nature of our faith
- Give solid reasons why we need other Christians, including children, in our corporate worship
- Describe simple steps to prepare for and treasure the Lord's Day

KEY IDEAS

- Christian corporate worship should be Word-centered, doxological, dialogical, simple, reverent, joy-filled, edifying, and verbal.
- Christians are not only saved unto God but also saved unto one another. We need one another.
- God knows our need for rest and has given us one day in seven to rest and worship.

REFLECTION & DISCUSSION QUESTIONS

Before the Video

What Do You Think?

Take a moment to answer the following questions. They will prepare you for the lecture.

- In the United States, how often do you imagine the average churchgoing Christian attends church?

- Should weekly church attendance be a priority for every Christian? Why or why not?

Scripture Reading

For just as the body is one and has many members, and all the members of the body, though many, are one body, so it is with Christ. For in one Spirit we were all baptized into one body—Jews or Greeks, slaves or free—and all were made to drink of one Spirit.

—1 Corinthians 12:12–13

- How does Paul describe the relationship of one person to another in Christ? How does that communicate the need that every Christian has for one another?

During the Video

Answer the following questions while you watch the video. They will guide you through the lecture.

Principles of Corporate Worship *0:00–10:14*

- Why ought worship to be simple and verbal? What does it mean for worship to be edifying? How might these two things connect?

- Do Christians need to gather with God's people on Sunday in corporate worship? Why or why not?

Gathering as a Whole Body to Worship *10:14–23:05*

- What are examples from Scripture that God's people are a gathering people?

- How does preparing for the Lord's Day assist us in corporate worship?

After the Video

Answer the following questions after you have finished the lecture. They will help you identify and summarize the major points.

- What are some of the principles of corporate worship described at the beginning of the lesson? Did any of the principles stand out as most valuable to you? If so, which ones? Why?

  If you are in a group, invite the members to share observations about the principles of worship. Ask: Which ones have you experienced or not experienced? Discuss how missing out on one principle or another would warp the experience of corporate worship.

- Why is it important to have young children welcomed into God's presence in worship?

  If you are in a group, ask the members whether they have experienced attending services as a child or as an adult with young children present. Ask: If so, what have you observed from your own experience or from engaging with children in this way? If not, what would you have missed out on?

- What steps can you take to more fully treasure the Lord's Day? Are there practical ways that you can prepare beforehand or establish new rhythms throughout the day itself?

  If you are in a group, discuss weekly rhythms around corporate worship. Ask whether people are often tired on Sunday mornings and how that affects their participation in worship and engagement in the Lord's Day. Help hold one another accountable for implementing one new change to treasure the next Lord's Day more fully.

PRAYER

Commit what you have learned from God's Word in this lesson to prayer.

- Praise God for the gift of the Lord's Day and the ability to worship Him with His people.
- Confess to God any sinful disregard for the Lord's Day or lack of willingness to engage in or prepare for corporate worship.

- Thank God for His design for the church to be composed of many members in one body and for the ways that He builds up your faith through the ministry of other believers.
- Ask God to give you a love for worshiping with His people and to help you engage with joy and with openness toward others, especially toward children.

REVIEW QUIZ

Use these multiple-choice questions to measure what you learned from this lesson.

1. Of the eight principles of worship named in this lesson, which one did the Reformers especially highlight as a necessary characteristic of corporate worship?
   a. Doxological
   b. Simple
   c. Joy-filled
   d. Edifying
2. In the United States today, how often does the average churchgoing Christian attend church?
   a. Occasionally
   b. Once a month
   c. Once a week
   d. Twice on Sundays
3. We are saved unto God, but we are also saved unto one another.
   a. True
   b. False
4. Which analogy does *not* define how God sees believers?
   a. Flock
   b. Building
   c. Lone Rangers
   d. Body
5. In Joel 2:15–16, whom did God call to assemble for corporate repentance?
   a. The people and the elders
   b. Children and nursing infants
   c. The bridegroom and the bride
   d. All of the above
6. Jesus' words "Let the little children come to me and do not hinder them, for to such belongs the kingdom of heaven" ought to inform our worship.
   a. True
   b. False

Answer Key—Created for Corporate Worship

REFLECTION & DISCUSSION QUESTIONS

Before the Video

What Do You Think?

These are personal questions. The answers should be based on your own knowledge and experience.

Scripture Reading

- How does Paul describe the relationship of one person to another in Christ? How does that communicate the need that every Christian has for one another?

  A body is one whole made up of many individual parts. Each part has a place where it belongs and where it functions to support the whole. Each part is needed to complete the body and to fulfill its individual role for the health and wholeness of the body. So in Christ, the body of believers is made up of many individual members who are each valuable and needed. Each member is given a gift to contribute to build up the whole body.

During the Video

Principles of Corporate Worship

- Why ought worship to be simple and verbal? What does it mean for worship to be edifying? How might these two things connect?

  The reason why worship ought to be simple and verbal flows out from its being Word-centered. Worship does not be adorned with props and show because we are focused on what we are hearing, and unnecessary adornment would be a distraction. Worship that is edifying builds up and equips the saints, encouraging our faith, and the best way to assure the edification of the saints is God's Word.

- Do Christians need to gather with God's people on Sunday in corporate worship? Why or why not?

  God's Word presents the case that Christians do need to gather for worship. In Scripture, many analogies help us understand the corporate nature of our faith. For example, God sees the church as a flock composed of many sheep that should be gathered for care, provision, protection, and direction. He also sees the church as a body made up of individual members who need one another, serve one another, and follow one Head—Jesus Christ. This is impossible if we are not gathering together.

Gathering as a Whole Body to Worship

- What are examples from Scripture that God's people are a gathering people?

  We are recreated as worshipers. This is seen profoundly from God's calling His people together to worship at the foot of Mount Sinai to the church's gathering to worship together regularly as recorded in Acts 2:42. This worship is something about which Paul instructed the church (see 1 Cor. 12–14), and he taught Timothy about Scripture's centrality in worship (see 1 Tim. 4:13), showing that there was a regularity to the worship of God's people. The author of Hebrews also clearly calls us not to neglect meeting together (10:26).

- How does preparing for the Lord's Day assist us in corporate worship?

  When we are tired, we may have difficulty fully engaging our hearts in worship or carefully paying attention to God's Word. Preparing to meet with God helps us worship more wholeheartedly and treasure the gift of time with God's people. If we prepare our minds, knowing what the Lord's Day is about, then we can also engage with God's people in a deeper way, having conversation about things like the sermon and what God is doing in another's life rather than about merely worldly or superficial things.

After the Video

- What are some of the principles of corporate worship described at the beginning of the lesson? Did any of the principles stand out as most valuable to you? If so, which ones? Why?

  The answers to these questions are personal in nature but do require you to recall the eight principles of corporate worship that were named: worship should be Word-centered, doxological, dialogical, simple, reverent, joy-filled, edifying, and verbal. Perhaps some of these principles have been a part of your worship experience for years, but you never thought of them on a conscious level. Actively thinking on these principles can help you appreciate worship and engage in it with more intentionality.

- Why is it important to have young children welcomed into God's presence in worship?

  In God's Word, we see many examples of God's calling His people, from the least to the greatest, to gather to worship Him. God's invitation of children into His presence highlights the importance that all of life is meant to be a life of worship. Children bear God's image as much as adults do, and they can glorify God with their lives and praise. By joining in worship, not only do children gain exposure to the truth about God and become accustomed to the rhythms of worship as they watch adults engage, but the adults also gain understanding about their role as children of God and can be encouraged and built up by a child's sincere faith. Children also help hold adults accountable for walking in obedience to God.

- What steps can you take to more fully treasure the Lord's Day? Are there practical ways that you can prepare beforehand or establish new rhythms throughout the day itself?

  Our attitude about corporate worship shades our experience of the gathering and affects those around us. Aim to come to worship with a grateful heart ready to worship in God's presence and to build up His people. Several practical ways to prepare for Sunday's worship service were offered in this lecture, beginning with a good night's rest on Saturday night, but the primary aim of this question is for you to reflect on your circumstances of your own life to make the most of the Lord's Day.

REVIEW QUIZ

1. **D.**
   The Reformers stressed that if worship services are not edifying for the believer, it is not true worship. Corporate worship is meant to encourage believers, build up their faith, and equip them to live by faith.

2. **B.**
   At the time this study was released, the average churchgoing Christian in the United States attended church once a month. This statistic should be staggering to us in light of God's call to us in worship and His worthiness to receive worship.

3. **A.**
   Rev. Helopoulos said, "We are saved unto God and we are saved unto one another. I need you, and you need me, and we need each other." This concept should encourage us more and more to gather together in worship.

4. **C.**
   The Lone Ranger is not one of the analogies that God uses for believers. Among other things, God sees them as a flock, as a building, and as a body. Many members make a whole, and each one is to be involved with the others.

5. **D.**
   God called the entire nation of Israel to repentance: "Blow the trumpet in Zion; consecrate a fast; call a solemn assembly; gather the people. Consecrate the congregation; assemble the elders; gather the children, even nursing infants. Let the bridegroom leave his room, and the bride her chamber" (Joel 2:15–16).

6. **A.**
   Jesus spoke these words to His disciples in Matthew 19:14, and they should bring us to deeper consideration about the importance of having children in worship. Worship is the high point of our week, and children should be present to sit under God's Word.

5

Corporate Worship: Reading & Preaching the Word

INTRODUCTION

Throughout history, God's people have regularly gathered to hear the Word of God and to respond to the Word of God. Faithfully, God works through His Word and the power of the Holy Spirit to draw people to salvation in Christ, to build the church, and to shape believers more and more into the image of Christ. In this lesson, Rev. Helopoulos helps us see that from the days of the first Apostles, Christian ministry has been centered on the public reading of Scripture and preaching from Scripture.

LEARNING GOALS

When you have finished this lesson, you should be able to:

- Discuss the historic, central role of God's Word in worship through reading and preaching
- Describe the dialogical aspect of worship as God speaks through His Word and we respond
- Identify three goals for listening well to the preaching of God's Word

KEY IDEAS

- In both the Old and New Testaments, God's people have gathered to hear the Word of God read and explained. Likewise, Christian corporate worship today is to be marked by the Word of God.
- Jesus sent out His disciples with "simply" the Holy Spirit and the Word of God—and now the gospel has spread to people on every continent of the earth.
- God has ordained to work in His people through His Word, by the power of the Holy Spirit, to shape and mold each believer more and more into the image of Jesus Christ.

REFLECTION & DISCUSSION QUESTIONS

Before the Video

What Do You Think?

Take a moment to answer the following questions. They will prepare you for the lecture.

- When evaluating corporate worship, how highly do you rank the charisma, intellect, and sense of humor of the preacher?

- Why is God's Word primarily communicated through preaching in Protestant corporate worship services instead through something like a question-and-answer format?

Scripture Reading

Until I come, devote yourself to the public reading of Scripture, to exhortation, to teaching.

—1 Timothy 4:13

- In this verse, the Apostle Paul is instructing Timothy. What does this guidance convey about the value of reading God's Word and preaching in corporate worship?

During the Video

Answer the following questions while you watch the video. They will guide you through the lecture.

Devoted to Reading and Preaching the Word *0:00–9:45*

- Why is the pulpit in the center of a church?

- What is *lectio continua* reading and preaching of the Word?

Power in Preaching *9:45–24:34*

- How does the Apostle Paul define what we call "preaching"? What is the main purpose of preaching?

- What type of word do we need and why?

- Do you think you can gain something from preaching by someone whom we don't esteem as a good or able preacher? Why or why not?

After the Video

Answer the following questions after you have finished the lecture. They will help you identify and summarize the major points.

- How does Paul's call to Timothy and Jesus' words of restoration to Peter connect to one another and relate to the ministry of the church today?

  If you are in a group, have group members read Acts 20:17–35. Ask: How do Paul's final words to the Ephesian elders expand on his call to Timothy and Jesus' words to Peter?

- What gives a Word-based ministry the potential to change lives?

  If you are in a group, consider the power of God's words in Scripture—for example, how God spoke to create or how many of Jesus' miracles involved speaking (to calm a storm, to heal lepers, to raise the dead). Ask: How should these affect the way that you think about listening to God's Word in worship?

- How do the three application points for listening well to God's Word being read and preached assist in strengthening the church and engaging in the experience of corporate worship?

  If you are in a group, ask the members to share about experiences with listening to preaching astutely, attentively, and responsively. Ask: What strategies have worked for you?

PRAYER

Commit what you have learned from God's Word in this lesson to prayer.

- Praise God for the power of His Word and His Spirit to bring life to your soul.
- Confess to God any resistance to submitting to His Word or lack of interest in hearing His Word read and preached in corporate worship.
- Thank God for the preacher(s) in your local church and in other ministries that are investing in your life.

- Ask God to bless those who are ministering to you through the Word and ask God to awaken your heart to hear His Word read and preached in worship so that you are made more like Christ.

REVIEW QUIZ

Use these multiple-choice questions to measure what you learned from this lesson.

1. We lean on a preacher's gifts for edification in worship.
   a. True
   b. False
2. The Lord Jesus Christ sent out His disciples with every worldly provision that they would need.
   a. True
   b. False
3. Good church architecture places the pulpit in the middle of the church. Why is this primarily?
   a. To assist the preacher in projecting his voice
   b. To help the congregation see the preacher
   c. To show that the Word of God is the center of our worship
   d. To avoid distractions within the congregation
4. In Scripture, which of the leaders listed below led God's people to gather to hear God's Word?
   a. Moses
   b. Ezra and Nehemiah
   c. Timothy
   d. All of the above
5. Who was used as a famous example of *lectio continua* preaching in this lecture?
   a. Heinrich Bullinger
   b. John Calvin
   c. Martin Luther
   d. Huldrych Zwingli
6. When the Apostle Paul wrote to Timothy, what two descriptions did he use for the practice of "preaching"?
   a. Spirit and Word
   b. Question and answer
   c. Teaching and exhortation
   d. Doxology and dialogue

Answer Key—Corporate Worship: Reading & Preaching the Word

REFLECTION & DISCUSSION QUESTIONS

Before the Video

What Do You Think?

These are personal questions. The answers should be based on your own knowledge and experience.

Scripture Reading

- In this verse, the Apostle Paul is instructing Timothy. What does this guidance convey about the value of reading God's Word and preaching in corporate worship?

  While Paul was away, the younger Timothy continued to conduct ministry, grow in his skill as a preacher, and gain new experiences in serving the local church. Paul exhorts Timothy to devote *himself to the Word of God when the church gathers, to let the Word lead the teaching and exhortation. A call to this type of devotion helps us understand how important the Word is in our worship..*

During the Video

Devoted to Reading and Preaching the Word

- Why is the pulpit in the center of a church?

  The architecture of the church building communicates to the congregation. Placing the pulpit in the front and center and often raised in a church's sanctuary is a visual demonstration of giving God's Word and the ministry of preaching the central place in the church's life and practice. Everything else revolves around the Word and is directed by the Word. This design reinforces the authority of God's Word and the submission of each believer to walk in obedience to it.

- What is *lectio continua* reading and preaching of the Word?

  Lectio continua *can refer both to the reading and preaching of the Word, but its meaning in reference to both is the same. A* lectio continua *approach to reading and preaching the Word means that we progress through Scripture verse by verse, week by week.*

Power in Preaching

- How does the Apostle Paul define what we call "preaching"? What is the main purpose of preaching?

  Paul spoke of preaching as "teaching" and "exhortation." The preaching follows the reading of the Word to simply explain the meaning of the Word, to give a sense of the text, and to make the meaning of the text clear. "Teaching" informs the mind to give a clear sense of the Word so that someone's thinking is shaped by the Word. As thinking is shaped by the Word, actions will be shaped by the Word. Preaching is meant to help someone understand the Word and apply it.

- What type of word do we need and why?

  In preaching, we hear a word from outside of us, and this is precisely what we need. Many voices vie for our attention, but we are finite and fallible. Who sees enough of reality to offer a comprehensive perspective? Whom can we trust to tell the truth? We need to hear from God, who knows all things. God's understanding is infinite, and He has provided His Word to lead and guide us. Our souls need to listen to Him and His Word, so that we will be shaped and molded by His truth.

- Do you think you can gain something from preaching by someone whom we don't esteem as a good or able preacher? Why or why not?

  We need to recognize that if a preacher opens God's Word, there is always something to be gained. God's Word is powerful to work in the lives of His saints. Even in the ministry of a simple, dull, or inexperienced preacher, God's Word can speak powerfully. Look to God's Word to learn, to grow, to be fed, and to be equipped for the walk of faith.

After the Video

- How does Paul's call to Timothy and Jesus' words of restoration to Peter connect to one another and relate to the ministry of the church today?

  Paul, in his first letter to Timothy, called him to "devote [himself] to the public reading of Scripture, to exhortation, to teaching" (4:13). Paul called Timothy to this because the Word is how God's people are fed. When Jesus restored Peter after his threefold denial, He asked him three times, "Do you love me?" and called Peter to "feed [His] sheep" (John 21:17). Paul's words to Timothy and Jesus' words to Peter can be taken together as a simple definition of Christian ministry: "Love the Lord, love His people, love His Word." God has ordained to work among His people by His Word, and therefore Christian ministry is to be centered on bringing the Word of God to His people as a way of loving Him and His people.

- What gives a Word-based ministry the potential to change lives?

  God's relationship with humans is reflective of His nature and ours; we are created in His image. Like God, we are real beings who exist with the capacity for relationships that share intellectual understanding, emotional interaction, and a spiritual dynamic. From God's example and our own experience, we see that relationships thrive in communication, and words are a key to this connection. Words spoken from one to another indicate proximity, relationship, and responsiveness. God's Word to His people indicates that He is drawing near and is present in their lives, that He has a relationship with them, and that He looks for their response to His Word. Scripture reveals that the words of God are powerful and active. His Word can connect with our minds to bring understanding, stir our emotions, and enliven our spirits so that our thoughts and feelings are shaped by God's Word and will fuel our actions according to God's Word.

- How do the three application points for listening well to God's Word being read and preached assist in strengthening the church and engaging in the experience of corporate worship?

  The call to listen astutely involves attention to the source of the preaching. Is it founded on the Word of God? Does it line up with the whole counsel of Scripture? If not, the preacher is not aligned with God's call for pastors to bring the Word of God to the people of God. The call to listen attentively involves an awareness of distraction and a decision to resist the temptation to lose track of the Word's message. When distractions come, do you bring your mind back to the Word? Are there practical steps you can take to help avoid distraction? Consider sitting near the front of the room, following along in your Bible with the preaching, or jotting simple notes on key points to help keep your mind focused. The call to be responsive is an invitation to rely on the Holy Spirit to bring understanding and to earnestly seek after what God has for you in His Word, regardless of critiques on the preacher himself.

REVIEW QUIZ

1. **B.**
   Our edification in corporate worship should come from the Spirit of God and the Word of God. The Spirit of God has chosen to work by the Word of God. This is an aspect of what it is to worship in spirit and in truth.

2. **B.**
   A key point in this lesson: "The Lord Jesus Christ sent out His disciples with His Word and His Spirit. The Spirit attends to the Word and the Word works with the Spirit." Jesus' disciples did not require wealth, power, or prestige to accomplish the work of spreading the gospel of the kingdom; they only needed God's Word and Spirit.

3. **C.**
   Good architecture places the pulpit in the middle of the church to show that the Word of God is the center of our worship. From here, God's primacy in worship and our dependence on Him is communicated. When the Lord's table is below the pulpit, this also communicates that God's Word governs the table.

4. **D.**
   The examples of Moses, Ezra, Nehemiah, and Timothy as men who called God's people together to hear God's Word were highlighted in this lecture. If we allow Scripture to inform our worship, then the reading of Scripture will be included in our worship.

5. **B.**
   The phrase lectio continua *indicates preaching through a whole book of the Bible, verse by verse, over the course of several Lord's Days. A famous example of this type of preaching is when Calvin returned to Geneva after a three-year hiatus, he resumed preaching right where he had left off.*

6. **C.**
   In 1 Timothy 4:13, Paul spoke of what we call "preaching" as "teaching" and "exhortation," which is a sober reminder that preaching should never become mere entertainment.

6

Corporate Worship: Singing & Praying the Word

INTRODUCTION

Along with reading the Word and preaching the Word, God's people also sing the Word and pray the Word in corporate worship. The content of the songs and the prayers is to reflect the truth of God's Word and in many cases may be adapted directly from Scripture. The songs and the prayers are also to be congregational so that all the people can join in singing praise to God and in praying together in God's presence.

LEARNING GOALS

When you have finished this lesson, you should be able to:

- Describe the role of singing in worship and the key considerations that should shape our congregational worship songs
- Discuss the role of prayer in worship, give historical examples of corporate prayer, and offer practical suggestions for prayer before, during, and after corporate worship

KEY IDEAS

- As far back as we can see, singing and prayer have been a part of the practice of corporate worship among God's people.
- Along with giving examples of many men and women worshiping in song and prayer, Scripture also provides a source of guidance for congregational worship in song and corporate prayer.
- Singing and praying are essential disciplines in the life of a Christian.

REFLECTION & DISCUSSION QUESTIONS

Before the Video

What Do You Think?

Take a moment to answer the following questions. They will prepare you for the lecture.

- Think of at least one worship song or hymn that you enjoy singing. What makes it meaningful to you?
- Before attending worship, do you spend time in prayer asking for God to be at work in the service? Why or why not?

Scripture Reading

Know that the Lord, he is God! It is he who made us, and we are his; we are his people, and the sheep of his pasture. Enter his gates with thanksgiving, and his courts with praise! Give thanks to him; bless his name!

—Psalm 100:3–4

- How does the mindset described at the beginning of this passage lay a foundation for entering God's presence in the manner that is commanded?

During the Video

Answer the following questions while you watch the video. They will guide you through the lecture.

A Crucial Element of Worship *0:00–11:23*

- How did Calvin describe the Psalms and why?
- What are some examples of the significance of singing and worship in the Psalms and in the lives of God's people?

Praying the Word *11:23–22:21*

- When we are not sure what to pray, what is one of the best ways to pray?

- What are some examples of how Jesus thought about the practice of corporate prayer?

After the Video

Answer the following questions after you have finished the lecture. They will help you identify and summarize the major points.

- What are some biblical examples of praise that were mentioned in this lesson from the New Testament?

  If you are in a group, ask the members to read excerpts from some of the songs of worship in Luke 1–2. Ask: What draws you to these passages? Discuss the context in which the songs were sung.

- What should mark our singing, songs, and the accompaniment to our voices?

  If you are in a group, invite the members to share about favorite hymns and why they are meaningful.

- How were those who think that they do not know how to pray encouraged in this lecture?

  If you are in a group, ask the members to highlight at least one application point they hope to put into practice to grow in prayer, particularly in prayer related to corporate worship. If time allows, pray together for growth in prayer in your corporate worship.

PRAYER

Commit what you have learned from God's Word in this lesson to prayer.

- Praise God for being worthy of our songs of praise and powerful to answer our prayers.
- Confess to God any lack of singing praise or any prayerlessness in your walk of faith.
- Thank God for the examples of Godward songs and prayers in Scripture that can shape our songs and prayers today.
- Ask God to bless your local church with an increased sense of His presence as you worship in song and in prayer.

REVIEW QUIZ

Use these multiple-choice questions to measure what you learned from this lesson.

1. Praise and worship includes a sense of reverence and awe.
   a. True
   b. False
2. What was called a "crucial" element of worship in this lecture?
   a. Prayer
   b. Preaching
   c. Sacraments
   d. Singing
3. In Colossians 3, the Apostle Paul says that we are to engage in what types of songs?
   a. Worshipful ballads
   b. Instrumental meditations
   c. Psalms, hymns, and spiritual songs
   d. All of the above
4. What did Charles Spurgeon call the "furnace of the church"?
   a. Three young men
   b. Saints gathered in prayer
   c. His anointed preaching
   d. Powerful corporate singing
5. What types of prayer should be part of corporate worship services?
   a. Prayers of invocation
   b. Prayers of thanksgiving
   c. Pastoral prayers
   d. All of the above
6. We draw near to God by prayer as He draws near to us by His Spirit.
   a. True
   b. False

Answer Key—Corporate Worship: Singing & Praying the Word

REFLECTION & DISCUSSION QUESTIONS

Before the Video

What Do You Think?

These are personal questions. The answers should be based on your own knowledge and experience.

Scripture Reading

- How does the mindset described at the beginning of this passage lay a foundation for entering God's presence in the manner that is commanded?

  Thinking on who God is and who we are prepares us to come to corporate worship with a thankful heart ready to give praise. God is our Creator; we are His creatures. He cares for us as a shepherd cares for his flock. This picture naturally suggests the specific ways that God has demonstrated His faithfulness and has met our needs. Therefore, we will have specific provisions for which to give thanks as we gather to worship.

During the Video

A Crucial Element of Worship

- How did Calvin describe the Psalms and why?

  Calvin called the Psalms "an anatomy of the soul" because everything that goes on within our souls, all the feelings that we have, all the different ways our souls are moved, can all be expressed through the Psalms.

- What are some examples of the significance of singing and worship in the Psalms and in the lives of God's people?

  The Psalms of Ascent were sung on pilgrimages to Jerusalem, and Psalm 15 and 24 are two of the psalms that we know were sung as people approached the gates of the temple. Additionally, singing accompanied the sacrifices that priests offered to God.

Praying the Word

- When we are not sure what to pray, what is one of the best ways to pray?

  One of the best ways to inform our prayers is to pray Scripture back to God. We can pray for the fulfillment of God's promises by quoting God's Word back to Him and asking for His faithful care and provision.

- What are some examples of how Jesus thought about the practice of corporate prayer?

  Jesus saw prayer as an essential element of worship among God's people. When He spoke of the temple, Jesus said that it was to be known as a "house of prayer for all the nations" (Mark 11:17). When Jesus taught His disciples to pray, He taught them to pray corporately with the Lord's Prayer through phrases such as "Our Father in heaven, . . . give us this day our daily bread, . . . and forgive us our debts, . . . and lead us not into temptation" (Matt. 6:9–13).

After the Video

- What are some biblical examples of praise that were mentioned in this lesson from the New Testament?

  Scripture bears witness to centuries of the praises of God's people. In God's Word, we see a glimpse into the exuberance of Mary in singing the "Magnificat" and Zechariah in his "Benedictus." We also find songs in the Epistles, such as found in Philippians 2:5–11 and Colossians 1:15–20. We can also see that singing was a part of the worship of the early church in various epistles (for examples, see 1 Cor. 14:26; Eph. 5:19).

- What should mark our singing, songs, and the accompaniment to our voices?

  Songs of worship are to be biblically informed, theologically accurate in light of the whole counsel of Scripture, and theologically profound to reflect the holy majesty of our glorious God. A song of worship is to engage our heart and mind. The tune should be simple enough for the congregation to sing together, with a melody that suits the emotion of the words; if instrumentation is added, it should not drown out the main instrument of praise that God seeks: the voices of His children.

- How were those who think that they do not know how to pray encouraged in this lecture?

  Although many Christians believe they should pray more than they do or feel inadequate in prayer, God welcomes our prayers and seeks them in times of corporate worship. Each of us will be a lifelong student in the school of prayer. We can grow by praying the prayers of Scripture and listening to the prayers of pastors and others. An important encouragement from this lesson: "Struggling in prayer is no shame; prayerlessness is. That is a shame. Let's be a praying people. It is just one of the great mercies of our God that He draws near to His people, that He loves to hear our cries, and that He cares. And we can go to Him with all of our sorrows, all of our joys, all of our elations, all of our deep valleys; and He listens, cares, and responds to our prayers."

REVIEW QUIZ

1. **A.**
   Praise and worship was described as a sense of awe and wonder. There are necessary elements of worship, and that is why worship is not merely a feeling, yet it must be engaged in from the heart.

2. **D.**
   While all of these are elements regulated to us for worship by Scripture, singing the Word was described as a "crucial" element of worship. Rev. Helopoulos said, "Singing is a crucial element of worship, and it has been among the people of God for as long as we can see." Though singing is not all that there is to worship, it is crucial for worship because it is how we fulfill the command to give praises to God.

3. **C.**
   "Let the word of Christ dwell in you richly, teaching and admonishing one another in all wisdom, singing psalms and hymns and spiritual songs, with thankfulness in your hearts to God" (Col. 3:16).

4. **B.**
   A story was shared of Spurgeon's showing "the furnace" to visitors of the church and bringing them to a room filled with saints on their knees in prayer for God to work in the worship service.

5. **D.**
   Many types of public prayer and private prayer should be evident in every corporate worship service. Private prayer is another crucial feature of our worship and should be a natural response to a Godward-focused heart in worship.

6. **A.**
   A key point in this lesson: "We draw near to God by prayer as He draws near to us by His Spirit. This is what God's people do." This is displayed powerfully in Solomon's dedication of the temple in 1 Kings 8 when after he prayer, the glory of God filled the temple.

7

Corporate Worship: The Sacraments

INTRODUCTION

Continuing the theme of living a life of worship, Rev. Helopoulos highlights the role of the sacraments in helping us to see the Word in corporate worship. In both the Old and New Testaments, God graciously provided visible signs to remind His people of His covenant promises to them. Throughout the centuries, these signs served as reassurance that the people belong to God and that He belongs to them.

LEARNING GOALS

When you have finished this lesson, you should be able to:

- Highlight the kindness of God in giving the sacraments of baptism and the Lord's Supper as a sign and seal of His covenant promises
- Discuss the inauguration of God's covenant with Abraham and how it points from Genesis 3 to the atoning death of Jesus Christ
- Describe the nature and purpose of the covenant signs given in both the Old and New Testaments

KEY IDEAS

- In Genesis 3:15, God's promise establishes the theme that unfolds in the rest of Scripture as God faithfully fulfills His Word.
- God's promise is formally inaugurated in the covenant with Abraham and reaffirmed at the Passover when God delivered the people of Israel from Egypt.
- After the coming of Christ, baptism and the Lord's Supper were given as signs and seals of God's new covenant with His people.

REFLECTION & DISCUSSION QUESTIONS

Before the Video

What Do You Think?

Take a moment to answer the following questions. They will prepare you for the lecture.

- In both the Old and New Testaments, why did God give signs of His covenant to His people? What purpose did they serve from one generation to the next?

- What meaning do you see behind the sacraments of baptism and the Lord's Supper? Do you find that practicing the sacraments with God's people affects your faith? Why or why not?

Scripture Reading

He [Abraham] received the sign of circumcision as a seal of the righteousness that he had by faith while he was still uncircumcised. The purpose was to make him the father of all who believe without being circumcised, so that righteousness would be counted to them as well.

—Romans 4:11

- When did Abraham receive the sign of circumcision? What did the sign symbolize?

During the Video

Answer the following questions while you watch the video. They will guide you through the lecture.

Reassurance of God's Promise *0:00–12:14*

- What must we be careful of when talking about the sacraments?

- How does God's call to Abraham relate to the *protoeuangelion*? What does God do for Abraham to assure him of His promises?

A Sign and Seal of the Covenant *12:14–25:45*

- How do the covenantal signs of the Old Testament and the sacraments of the New Testament relate to the cross of Jesus Christ?

- How do the feast of the Passover and the sacrament of the Lord's Supper draw our eyes to the Lord Jesus?

After the Video

Answer the following questions after you have finished the lecture. They will help you identify and summarize the major points.

- While Abraham was waiting for the fulfillment of God's promises, he asked for a sign to reassure him of God's commitment to fulfill His Word. What are believers waiting for today, and how do the sacraments serve as a sign of God's faithfulness to bring His Word to pass?

  If you are in a group, ask the members to discuss their participation in the sacraments of baptism and the Lord's Supper. Ask: How does participation in corporate worship affect your personal faith? What do these signs help the congregation to "see"?

- What is a covenant? How is God's covenant with Abraham unique? What does God's role in this covenant tell you about God?

  If you are in a group, have the members read Genesis 15 and Jeremiah 34:17–20. Ask: How does the passage in Jeremiah help you understand what is happening in Genesis 15?

- How do the sacraments act as a seal for our faith?

  If you are in a group, ask the members to share their experiences of baptism and the Lord's Supper. Ask: What do these signs mean on a personal level? Take time to reflect and give thanks to God for His kindness.

PRAYER

Commit what you have learned from God's Word in this lesson to prayer.

- Praise God for His kindness and grace in providing the sacraments as a visible sign of His covenant with His people.

- Confess to God any disdain for those who disagree with your view of the sacraments and any prideful urge to debate uncharitably over these matters.
- Thank God for His faithfulness to fulfill His promise in Genesis 3 and to care for His people through the centuries of waiting for its ultimate fulfillment.
- Ask God to bless your engagement in the sacraments of baptism and the Lord's Supper in corporate worship.

REVIEW QUIZ

Use these multiple-choice questions to measure what you learned from this lesson.

1. If we become engrossed in a debate about the sacraments, what might we miss?
   a. Considering the depth of God's kindness
   b. Understanding the graciousness of God
   c. Marveling at God's knowledge of our frame and need for reassurance
   d. All of the above

2. In Genesis 3:15, what is the *protoeuangelion*?
   a. The story of the fall
   b. The first declaration of the gospel
   c. The curse on the man and the woman
   d. The curse on the serpent

3. What did Augustine call the sacraments?
   a. The visible Word
   b. A sign and seal
   c. Reassurance of the promises
   d. A prop for our faith

4. What does the rite of baptism signify?
   a. The putting away of the flesh
   b. Being washed and renewed
   c. Being born again
   d. All of the above

5. The sacraments are more than mere signs.
   a. True
   b. False

6. Which of the following is God's great covenant promise that is seen in the sacraments?
   a. "I will give you a new heart, and a new spirit I will put within you" (Ezek. 36:26).
   b. "I will put my law within them, and I will write it on their hearts" (Jer. 31:33).
   c. "I will walk among you and will be your God, and you shall be my people" (Lev. 26:12).
   d. "I am with you always, to the end of the age" (Matt. 28:20).

Answer Key—Corporate Worship: The Sacraments

REFLECTION & DISCUSSION QUESTIONS

Before the Video

What Do You Think?

These are personal questions. The answers should be based on your own knowledge and experience.

Scripture Reading

- When did Abraham receive the sign of circumcision? What did the sign symbolize?

  First, Abraham believed God's promises and received the righteousness that comes by faith. Then God gave him the sign of circumcision as evidence of what God had done in calling Abraham to Himself and promising His care and provision to Abraham. Circumcision became a sign of belonging to God and of waiting for the fulfillment of His promises.

During the Video

Reassurance of God's Promise

- What must we be careful of when talking about the sacraments?

  Talking about the sacraments can often lead to such a debate on the nature of the sacraments themselves that Christians overlook the great kindness of God in giving the sacraments. Thus, this lesson focuses on God's giving of the signs of the covenant to show God's goodness in both the Old and New Testaments in providing a seal for His promises.

- How does God's call to Abraham relate to the *protoeuangelion*? What does God do for Abraham to assure him of His promises?

  The protoeuangelion *is the first gospel proclamation that we find in Scripture. After Adam and Eve ate of the forbidden tree, God cursed the ground and the serpent but also promised that someone would come to crush the head of the serpent. God's calling out Abraham from Ur in Genesis 12 is an advancement of this promise in Scripture, as God promises him a child. By the time of Genesis 15, Abraham was still childless and asked God to reassure him of His promise, and that's when God entered into covenant with Abraham.*

A Sign and Seal of the Covenant

- How do the covenantal signs of the Old Testament and the sacraments of the New Testament relate to the cross of Jesus Christ?

  In the Old Testament, the covenantal signs of circumcision and the Passover point toward the fulfillment of God's promises to His people and to the coming of redemption through Jesus Christ. In the New Testament, the sacraments of baptism and the Lord's Table point back to reflect on Christ's life, death, and resurrection.

- How do the feast of the Passover and the sacrament of the Lord's Supper draw our eyes to the Lord Jesus?

  The meaning of the feast of the Passover has clear parallels with the Lord's Supper, which Jesus established with His disciples during the feast of the Passover and on the night that He was arrested and crucified. Just as the sacrificial Passover lamb was slain and its blood was spread on a doorpost to save a household from death in Egypt, so Jesus would be slain and shed His blood to rescue His children from the destruction of sin and death. Just as the Passover lamb was eaten so that it gave its life and strength to the household, so we partake of Jesus when eating the bread and drinking the cup of the Lord's Supper.

After the Video

- While Abraham was waiting for the fulfillment of God's promises, he asked for a sign to reassure him of God's commitment to fulfill His Word. What are believers waiting for today, and how do the sacraments serve as a sign of God's faithfulness to bring His Word to pass?

  Today, God's people are waiting for the second coming of Christ, and the sacraments of baptism and the Lord's Supper both point toward the realities to come. We await God's fulfillment of His promises to us for the resurrection of the dead and the gift of eternal life with Christ in heaven. Baptism points to the promise of resurrection in Christ, that we will be eternally safe in God's care and live by His resurrection power. The Lord's Supper points toward the coming kingdom of God and the celebration of the marriage of Christ and His Bride. Both sacraments point toward our place of belonging to God and His promises belonging to us.

- What is a covenant? How is God's covenant with Abraham unique? What does God's role in this covenant tell you about God?

  A covenant is formed when two or more parties come together to agree on something and bind themselves to fulfill a certain matter. God's covenant with Abraham was unique in that God made the covenant with Himself; Abraham did not take part in the covenant ceremony, though God was truly covenanting with him. Because suzerain and vassal covenantal arrangements were normal in the ancient Near East, this feature of God's covenant with Abraham would have been astounding, even to Abraham. By passing through the cut animal pieces, God promised to take on the curses of the covenant regardless of the faithfulness of the other party. In addition to the dimensions of God's character that you might have highlighted in relation to his role in this covenant, one thing that certainly can be seen is God's faithfulness to His people.

- How do the sacraments act as a seal for our faith?

  A wax seal on a letter gives evidence to the authenticity of the letter's contents. In the same way, the sacraments act as a seal for us and invite us to engage with God's covenant personally, to take part through our actions and our faith and to receive His gift of a place among His people. Participating in baptism and partaking of the Lord's Supper demonstrate our enfolding into the people of God and give us a sign of reassurance that we belong to God and that He belongs to us. They act as a seal on our faith by impressing us with the mark of the people of God.

REVIEW QUIZ

1. **D.**
   Debates about the sacraments can overshadow the depth of God's kindness, hiding the graciousness of God and leaving us without a recognition of God's care for our needs. We must take care not to lose these dimensions of the sacraments when talking about them with others.

2. **B.**
   The protoeuangelion *in Genesis 3:15 is the first declaration of the gospel: "I will put enmity between you and the woman, and between your offspring and her offspring; he shall bruise your head, and you shall bruise his heel."*

3. **A.**
   Although the other descriptions were mentioned in the lesson, Augustine called the sacraments "the visible Word." In worship we hear, sing, pray, and see *the Word.*

4. **D.**
   Baptism symbolizes many things, including but not limited to the putting away of the flesh, being born again, and being washed and renewed. Romans 6:4 tells us that we are united to Christ's death and resurrection through baptism.

5. **A.**
   The sacraments point to redemptive realities as signs, but they also seal those realities to us. When we partake of them in faith, they are real means of grace to us through which God confirms His promises to us.

6. **C.**
   "The signs of the covenant show that we belong to God and that He belongs to us." This reality is particularly seen in God's great covenant promise to dwell among His people in such places as Leviticus 26:12 and in the context of the great new covenant promises in Jeremiah (see 31:34) and Ezekiel (see 36:28), also giving us a striking way of understanding Jesus' promise that He is with us always.

8

Created for Family Worship: Why?

INTRODUCTION

As Christians, we may try to center life on Christ, but all too often, we do far less than we intend to. In this lesson, Rev. Helopoulos discusses how the practice of family worship makes great strides toward this goal. Family worship involves gathering with those of your household for a brief time of reading God's Word, prayer, and singing—ideally daily. The rhythm of focusing on God and adoring Him together is a key to living a life of worship.

LEARNING GOALS

When you have finished this lesson, you should be able to:

- Explain what family worship is
- Identify two main reasons for implementing family worship
- Discuss how family worship influences all those in the home, especially children, and opens opportunities for spiritual conversations with those closest to you

KEY IDEAS

- The practice of family worship involves taking just a few minutes to gather, read a portion of Scripture, pray, and sing together. It's not meant to be a burden.
- Family worship gives the opportunity to preserve the stories of God's work and to proclaim them among those living side by side in the household.
- Consistently putting the household in the way of God's means of grace will bear the fruit of God's grace at work in each person's life.

REFLECTION & DISCUSSION QUESTIONS

Before the Video

What Do You Think?

Take a moment to answer the following questions. They will prepare you for the lecture.

- What would be gained by gathering with the members of your household to read the Word, pray, and sing together for a few minutes each day?

- In daily life, what stands in the way of gathering for family worship? What outcome would make it worth scheduling around it?

Scripture Reading

He established a testimony in Jacob and appointed a law in Israel, which he commanded our fathers to teach to their children, that the next generation might know them, the children yet unborn, and arise and tell them to their children, so that they should set their hope in God.

—Psalm 78:5–7

- Whom did God command to teach about His testimony in Jacob? What is at stake if the command isn't obeyed?

During the Video

Answer the following questions while you watch the video. They will guide you through the lecture.

The Why *of Family Worship* — *0:00–12:56*

- What is the practice of family worship? Is it only for parents with young children?

- What are the two main reasons for gathering for family worship?

The What *of Family Worship* — *12:56–21:53*

- What three things do you do in family worship?

- How often do you need to practice family worship for it to be effective?

After the Video

Answer the following questions after you have finished the lecture. They will help you identify and summarize the major points.

- What are some reason why family worship is neglected?

  If you are in a group, ask the members to reflect on their experience of family worship. If it is something that they have practiced, ask: When did you have family worship, and how did you go about it?

- What does family worship help children to see about the Bible and why it that important?

  If you are in a group, invite the members to share experiences with children and Bible stories—perhaps a favorite Bible story recalled from childhood, an example of engaging with children over a Bible story at church or another setting, or something encountered as a parent raising children.

- What was Rev. Helopoulos' story about his son intended to communicate?

  If you are in a group, discuss your observations about this story. Ask: Does this type of engagement motivate you to begin implementing family worship in your home? Why or why not?

PRAYER

Commit what you have learned from God's Word in this lesson to prayer.

- Praise God for the gift of family worship and the invitation to share a Godward focus with others in your home.
- Confess to God any lack of initiative or courage leading to a neglect of family worship.
- Thank God for all the fathers and mothers who have spoken of His goodness through the ages so that you cherish Christ; thank Him for the next generation who need to hear about Him.
- Ask God to give you His vision for your engagement in family worship and for the wisdom and courage to be faithful to gather and share a Godward moment each day.

REVIEW QUIZ

Use these multiple-choice questions to measure what you learned from this lesson.

1. What was the main point of the story about the young boy in Ms. Scarwood's class?
   a. Children should be a part of corporate worship as well as family worship.
   b. Children should be a part of family worship as a training ground for corporate worship.
   c. Children can begin to see themselves as part of God's story through family worship.
   d. Family worship is critical for the faith of the family and affects our society at large.

2. If you miss a night or two or three, should you give up altogether?
   a. Yes, you've lost your chance.
   b. No, but you need to work a lot harder.
   c. No, just simply start again.
   d. No, but feel guilty about it.

3. We are to be, as Jonathan Edwards said, "a little church in our families."
   a. True
   b. False

4. Who wrote Psalm 78?
   a. The Sons of Korah
   b. Solomon
   c. David
   d. Asaph

5. In Psalm 78, what does the psalmist want to preserve?
   a. Hope in God
   b. The praise of God's people
   c. Who God is and what He has done
   d. All of the above

6. The two key reasons for having family worship are centering the home on Christ and passing on the faith to children.
   a. True
   b. False

Answer Key—Created for Family Worship: Why?

REFLECTION & DISCUSSION QUESTIONS

Before the Video

What Do You Think?

These are personal questions. The answers should be based on your own knowledge and experience.

Scripture Reading

- Whom did God command to teach about His testimony in Jacob? What is at stake if the command isn't obeyed?

  This verse declares that God commanded "our fathers" to teach their children about God's law and His testimonies. Can you imagine if those who experienced God's work in Jacob's, Moses', and David's day had not told anyone about it, let alone their children? We have gained so much through the obedience of those who have told others what God has done. Each generation has an opportunity to see and savor God's work and to tell of what they have seen and savored. The knowledge and faith of the next generation is at stake if no one opens his or her mouth. May we tell of the testimonies and the law, that they might "set their hope in God."

During the Video

The Why *of Family Worship*

- What is the practice of family worship? Is it only for parents with young children?

  The practice of family worship involves gathering the members of the household together to share in a brief time of worship together. This meeting involves all the people in the home—husband and wife, parents and children, a group of roommates, or any extended family members or friends who live under the same roof.

- What are the two main reasons for gathering for family worship?

  The two key reasons for family worship: (1) to center the home on Christ and (2) to pass on the faith to the next generation. People spend a lot of time at home with the people they love most. What a gift it is to engage together in worship with the aim of preserving what we have heard of who God is and what He has done and to proclaim it among our families and household.

The What *of Family Worship*

- What three things do you do in family worship?

  The household gathers simply to (1) read the Word, (2) pray, and (3) sing. Specific content is up to the family, but keeping things simple, short, and straightforward is helpful. We should not be striving to overachieve. Family worship is a very basic time together for a few minutes of worship.

- How often do you need to practice family worship for it to be effective?

  It's a good goal to have family worship each day, but it is likely that you won't do it each and every day all the time. Keep in mind that each time you gather, it makes a difference. It's worthwhile. If you miss a day or two or more, give yourself grace to start again fresh and gather as often as you can in a week. If something isn't working well, adjust and try again.

After the Video

- What are some reason why family worship is neglected?

  This discomfort that many feel when considering what it would be like to start family worship in their household draws attention to how much this discipline has been neglected. While some families do still regularly meet for family worship, it is not widespread. If a family has made it a priority, they are likely connecting in other ways as well and have made a determined decision to prioritize time together and to intentionally build their connections. Over the past decades in the United States, we have unfortunately witnessed the decline of the family and the church in general. Family members are often expected to disperse to their own pursuits instead of gathering for a single purpose. This lack of connectedness in the home affects every other sphere of life, and it causes much to slide into disrepair.

- What does family worship help children to see about the Bible and why it that important?

  Family worship provides an opportunity for children to see the faith of their parents as they respond to God's Word and share it with them. This time together opens a door for children to talk about Bible stories as real and true events, to ask questions, and to be encouraged to respond to what they hear. God intends for children to hear His testimonies and to know how He has acted throughout the ages so that they might "set their hope in [Him]." We must remember that God enjoys hearing the praise of children. When children see the faith of the men and women of Scripture as they go to God in prayer, worship Him, and obey (or disobey) Him, the children can make applications to their own lives and experiences.

- What was Rev. Helopoulos' story about his son intended to communicate?

  In Rev. Helopoulos' experience, family worship helped open his son's heart to speak about personal issues that he might not have been able to verbalize without it. As a result of family worship, he had more awareness of his son and could take a fatherly moment of care because of what they had shared. This shows how regular engagement in family worship can help open the doors of communication within the household. True, communication may never be easy, but having opportunities to talk about a vast range of topics makes deeper relationships more accessible. Family members can share from the readings and prayer and songs of worship, and these topics can springboard into something deeper at any moment. Spending time together allows households—especially parents—to have an understanding of what each person is going through and an alertness to that person's spiritual state.

REVIEW QUIZ

1. **C.**
   A story was told about a young five-year-old boy who told an enthralling story of Samuel in the Bible. His story was detailed and long, and the reason why he knew the story so well is because he understood that, in a sense, the story was about him. He was able to connect to the story to the larger story of redemption, even his personal redemption, and family worship can help instill this sense in a child.

2. **C.**
   If you miss a few nights of family worship, then simply start again. There is no reason to burden yourself with guilt; you shouldn't have to belabor regaining lost ground.

3. **A.**
   Jonathan Edwards said that we are "a little church in our families." If this is the case, then our homes ought to be a place of worship just as the church is a place of worship.

4. **D.**
   While David wrote the majority of psalms, Asaph penned Psalm 78, and in it, he calls us to preserve the testimonies of God's work and to proclaim it to the next generation. Asaph's call to us is God's call to us.

5. **D.**
   In Psalm 78, we see Asaph seeking to preserve the testimony of who God is and what He has done, along with the praise of God's people and their hope in God. Hope and praise ought to flow from reflecting on God's work, and family worship provides a consistent opportunity to do so.

6. **A.**
   In this lesson, one of the key reasons for having family worship is to pass on the faith to children, but even in a household with no children, the worship of God in the home helps center the household on Jesus Christ, the other key reason for family worship.

9

Created for Family Worship: How?

INTRODUCTION

Many evangelicals are not familiar with the practice of family worship, and they feel intimidated by the prospect. Because they have not experienced it, the unknown fosters disbelief that it can be achieved. Often people envision a much more formalized production than a simple gathering of the household to read a passage of Scripture, to pray together, and to sing. In this lesson, Rev. Helopoulos highlights practical tips for how to go about family worship and solid reasons for making the effort.

LEARNING GOALS

When you have finished this lesson, you should be able to:

- Give examples for a simple implementation of family worship
- Describe how family worship facilitates the peace of the home, the faith of children, and the health of the local church
- Identify attitudes and practices that will help your household implement regular family worship

KEY IDEAS

- The members of your household are meant to be together to help one another. Family worship provides a space in which to support and encourage one another.
- Family worship can be conducted simply and consistently.
- The content of family worship should be appropriate for the ages of the people represented in the household but should always include reading from the Bible.

REFLECTION & DISCUSSION QUESTIONS

Before the Video

What Do You Think?

Take a moment to answer the following questions. They will prepare you for the lecture.

- Before undertaking this study, what was your understanding of family worship? What did you imagine that it involved?

- What kind of effect do you think the regular practice of family worship would have on your close relationships? On husbands and wives? On siblings or roommates?

Scripture Reading

I am reminded of your sincere faith, a faith that dwelt first in your grandmother Lois and your mother Eunice and now, I am sure, dwells in you as well.

—2 Timothy 1:5

- In Timothy's life, who influenced his faith? How does the this give us inspiration in the practice of family worship?

During the Video

Answer the following questions while you watch the video. They will guide you through the lecture.

Family Worship Can Be Easy *0:00–9:32*

- How is Timothy's experience a simple lesson about how God works in our own lives?

- In the examples that were given of family worship, what was emphasized?

Purposes for Family Worship and How to Do It *9:32–24:57*

- What are some of the benefits of worshiping together as a family?

- What are the practical aspects of implementing family worship? How is it done?

After the Video

Answer the following questions after you have finished the lecture. They will help you identify and summarize the major points.

- Getting started in family worship can be intimidating. What obstacles were addressed in this lesson?

  If you are in a group, discuss common conceptions about family worship. Ask: Did this lesson help clarify a practical understanding of family worship? If so, how? If group members are not yet practicing family worship, do they think it would be possible for their household to begin?

- When households are engaged in family worship, it affects their local church. Recalling from the lesson, what are some of the benefits that the church will experience?

  If you are in a group, invite the members to share observations of how family worship can build up the local church. Ask: Does it seem like too much to center all your life on your worship experience? Why or why not?

- When a household begins to hold family worship, how can it keep the momentum going? What if some members lose interest?

  If you are in a group, ask whether the members have had experience with pushing through a lull in family devotions or in other areas of life. Ask: What has helped you regain and maintain healthy rhythms? Have the group share ideas and encouragement for getting through difficult times.

PRAYER

Commit what you have learned from God's Word in this lesson to prayer.

- Praise God for His means of grace to you through the people in your life and the privilege to gather for worship together.
- Confess to God any pride or guilt that has marked your experience in family worship and hindered you from receiving His good gifts.
- Thank God for the specific people who shared the gospel with you and for the people with whom you can share the gospel.

- Ask God for grace to practice family worship and for the deepening of your faith, your relationships, and your engagement in the local church through it.

REVIEW QUIZ

Use these multiple-choice questions to measure what you learned from this lesson.

1. Whose family is being referenced in this quote: "I am reminded of your sincere faith, a faith that dwelt first in your grandmother Lois and your mother Eunice and now, I am sure, dwells in you as well"?
   a. Paul's
   b. Peter's
   c. Timothy's
   d. James'
2. What did Rev. Helopoulos learn about family worship when he was candidating to be a pastor?
   a. All children should have their own Bibles.
   b. Always invite guests in your home to join you.
   c. It's best to have family worship after dinner.
   d. It can be easy.
3. The people in our lives are there by accident, and family worship brings our relationships purpose.
   a. True
   b. False
4. What is the best time for family worship?
   a. After breakfast
   b. During Sunday lunch
   c. Just before bedtime
   d. Whatever works for your household
5. If your household is distracted and unruly during family worship, how should you respond?
   a. Make sure they have to sit twice as long as usual.
   b. Recognize when it's time to wrap up, and just try again the next day.
   c. Fret over the failure, and try harder to be perfect.
   d. Make a few more rules to help everyone.
6. It encourages Christian character when you practice family worship.
   a. True
   b. False

Answer Key—Created for Family Worship: How?

REFLECTION & DISCUSSION QUESTIONS

Before the Video

What Do You Think?

These are personal questions. The answers should be based on your own knowledge and experience.

Scripture Reading

- In Timothy's life, who influenced his faith? How does the this give us inspiration in the practice of family worship?

  Here the Apostle Paul highlights Timothy's spiritual heritage that follows the line of his grandmother and mother, Lois and Eunice. Paul recognizes that the faith of one generation has influenced the next, and indeed, the same sincere faith of one and two has now found a home in another.

During the Video

Family Worship Can Be Easy

- How is Timothy's experience a simple lesson about how God works in our own lives?

  While each coming-to-faith testimony is unique, God works through similar means to draw His children to Himself. The story of Timothy's family can encourage us to invest in the spiritual nurturing of others in our own household through the practice of family worship. We are in one another's lives for a reason. God works through us and other people. This simple truth is especially poignant when we reflect on the individual who God used to bring the gospel to us.

- In the examples that were given of family worship, what was emphasized?

  Rev. Helopoulos shared examples of how simple and easy family worship can be. He described the surprise and relief found by parents who realize how basic the structure and implementation can be. There is no need for elaborate planning or lengthy gatherings. Family worship should incorporate reading, prayers, and singing that fits into the household's age range and aptitudes, without belaboring the worship.

Purposes for Family Worship and How to Do It

- What are some of the benefits of worshiping together as a family?

  Investing in family worship affects how the members of the household relate to one another and engage together. It encourages families to live out God-honoring character with one another in the home. Regularly gathering together holds each one accountable for resolving differences, and the peace in the home increases. Family worship also gives a family common knowledge from which to engage in further conversation and thus deepen relationships.

- What are the practical aspects of implementing family worship? How is it done?

  Practical tips for family worship include using the Bible for Scripture reading (everyone should have a Bible in hand) and hymnals for singing, meeting consistently at a time that works best for your household, gathering in the same place where distractions are minimal, engaging with good attitudes of joy and perseverance, and remembering to be flexible and have faith that it will be worthwhile despite varying attention spans or unexpected obstacles.

After the Video

- Getting started in family worship can be intimidating. What obstacles were addressed in this lesson?

  The sense of being overwhelmed by family worship could be dispelled by recognizing how simply it may be done. Do not put pressure on yourself or your family to overachieve. By taking simple steps, especially when getting started, you can aim to establish the new routine. We also need to identify the time that works best for our households and make our gatherings consistent. Meeting at the same time and same place helps each person become accustomed to family worship and begin to anticipate it as a natural part of the schedule.

- When households are engaged in family worship, it affects their local church. Recalling from the lesson, what are some of the benefits that the church will experience?

  Family worship benefits the local church because the household members are strengthened by spiritual engagement throughout the week. They are more prepared to engage in corporate worship. Children especially gain in corporate worship settings if they have become familiar with aspects of worship at home and they recognize that worship is for them. Singing in the home leads to stronger singing at church. Households that have worked out relational struggles are more ready to worship and engage in meeting the needs of others. Since the members have been strengthened in Christian character, they will be better equipped to interact with integrity in the body of Christ.

- When a household begins to hold family worship, how can it keep the momentum going? What if some members lose interest?

  As time passes, family worship will become routine, and you will encounter varied responses and experiences in the course of your time together. Sometimes children are distracted, and you just need to be content to wrap things up and move on. Don't lose heart, but gather again the next time. The moments of deeper engagement, and even extended conversation or reading, will come as well. Be flexible with the ebb and flow of life and what you are facing as a household. Overall, families find that keeping things simple is best and that starting slow and steady will win in the end.

REVIEW QUIZ

1. **C.**
   The Apostle Paul wrote these words in 2 Timothy 1:5. Paul's relationship as a spiritual father to Timothy also teaches us the principle of passing down the faith to future generations, something for which family worship is particularly well suited.
2. **D.**
   Rev. Helopoulos had a more expanded idea of family worship, and when he saw it in practice with a family, he realized how very simple and easy it could be.
3. **B.**
   "The people in our lives are not an accident." The Lord put you together in order for you to help one another. Family worship is an arena where this can be lived out.
4. **D.**
   The time that works best for your household is the right time. There is no "wrong" time; just choose what works well for you. Trying to force an unnatural time and having family worship in a unhelpful setting may lead only to greater frustration.
5. **B.**
   Sometimes it's best to recognize when it's time to wrap up and try again the next day. There is grace and flexibility for the good nights and the bad nights. Anticipate a mix of attention spans and levels of engagement.
6. **A.**
   One of the benefits of family worship is that it encourages everyone to practice Christian character. Meeting regularly together provides accountability for behaving well in ordinary daily interactions.

10

Created for Private Worship

INTRODUCTION

The final sphere of worship in this study is the sphere of private worship or secret worship. We see the priority of private worship displayed in the lives of many in Scripture. From Joshua and Daniel in the Old Testament to the Apostle Peter and the Lord Jesus Himself in the New Testament, Rev. Helopoulos helps us see our need for private worship. There we abide in the presence of God through time in the Word and prayer, becoming more like Him in the process.

LEARNING GOALS

When you have finished this lesson, you should be able to:

- Discuss the value of practicing private worship regularly
- Identify the main elements of private worship
- Describe steps to take to renew devotional life when it becomes dry

KEY IDEAS

- Throughout history, we see God's people investing in private times of meditating on God's Word, praying to God, and pouring out their hearts to Him.
- Private worship is a time to draw near to God in the Word and prayer, to dwell in His presence, and to be transformed more and more to be like Jesus.
- When private worship becomes dry, we should continue to press on, bring the dryness to God, ask for His renewal, and meditate on Scripture about Christ until our affections for Him are stirred.

REFLECTION & DISCUSSION QUESTIONS

Before the Video

What Do You Think?

Take a moment to answer the following questions. They will prepare you for the lecture.

- What are some examples in Scripture of people taking time alone for meditating on God's Word and prayer?

- What role does private worship play in the lives of Christians today? Is personal time for prayer and God's Word a priority in your life? Why or why not?

Scripture Reading

And when you pray, you must not be like the hypocrites. For they love to stand and pray in the synagogues and at the street corners, that they may be seen by others. Truly, I say to you, they have received their reward. But when you pray, go into your room and shut the door and pray to your Father who is in secret. And your Father who sees in secret will reward you.

—Matthew 6:5–6

- What reason does Jesus give for why hypocrites love to pray in public? When Jesus instructs us to pray in private, what reasoning does He give for our motivation?

During the Video

Answer the following questions while you watch the video. They will guide you through the lecture.

The Value of Private Worship *0:00–10:27*

- Who in Scripture do we see practicing private worship? In these examples, what is involved in seeking God's presence in secret?

- Why do Christians seek to pull away and have time alone with God? What is accomplished during this time?

Practical Ways to Invest in Private Worship *10:27–24:38*

- What practical steps can you take to establish a habit of private worship? What should that time include?

- If you experience dryness in private worship, what can you do to seek refreshment and renewal?

After the Video

Answer the following questions after you have finished the lecture. They will help you identify and summarize the major points.

- What is private worship? What do we gain by spending this time with God?

  If you are in a group, discuss the process of developing a habit of daily devotions. Have the members share their experiences with private worship. Ask: How have you seen the benefits grow over time?

- Recalling the story of Jesus' interaction with Mary and Martha, what had Martha done? Why did Jesus commend Mary's choice? What does this story teach us?

  If you are in a group, invite the members to share any experiences they have had with being busy with kingdom work and not busy about the King. Ask the members to share reflections on experiences in which they were reminded of the priority of their relationship with God over efforts of practical service.

- What does your practice of private worship look like?

  If you are in a group, ask whether the members have ever experienced dryness in their devotional life and what they did to overcome it.

PRAYER

Commit what you have learned from God's Word in this lesson to prayer.

- Praise God for the gift of coming into His presence in private worship to abide in His Word and prayer.
- Confess to God your need for renewal and transformation in His presence; confess any sinful resistance to meeting with Him in private worship.

- Thank God for the way that Jesus taught us to pray in secret sincerity and showed us how to be alone in communion with God.
- Ask God for grace to faithfully set apart space for private worship in your life and to help other believers do the same.

REVIEW QUIZ

Use these multiple-choice questions to measure what you learned from this lesson.

1. Which man in the Old Testament did God directly command to meditate on His law day and night?
   a. David
   b. Abraham
   c. Moses
   d. Joshua
2. In the New Testament, who rose up early and went out to a quiet place alone for prayer?
   a. Peter
   b. Jesus
   c. Cornelius
   d. Paul
3. Perfection is the mark of the Christian life.
   a. True
   b. False
4. Faithfully spending time in God's presence in the Word and prayer was likened to which of the following?
   a. Sowing seeds to reap a future harvest
   b. Building a city one brick at a time
   c. Planting an acorn and planning for the oak tree
   d. All of the above
5. Which African proverb was shared to highlight our need to meet with God regularly in private worship?
   a. "Don't be a Martha."
   b. "No day dawns like another."
   c. "Brother, the grass grows on your path."
   d. "Little and lasting is better than much and passing."
6. What were the three spheres of worship in a life of worship compared to?
   a. A threefold cord
   b. A three-leaf clover
   c. A three-legged stool
   d. A three-ring binder

Answer Key—Created for Private Worship

REFLECTION & DISCUSSION QUESTIONS

Before the Video

What Do You Think?

These are personal questions. The answers should be based on your own knowledge and experience.

Scripture Reading

- What reason does Jesus give for why hypocrites love to pray in public? When Jesus instructs us to pray in private, what reasoning does He give for our motivation?

  Jesus sees that hypocrites are motivated to pray in synagogues and on street corners not because they want to pray to God but because they want to be seen by others. This insincere behavior does not bring God's blessing but the temporary "reward" of being seen. Jesus calls us to go to pray in secret, knowing that our heavenly Father will see us and hear us in prayer. God will reward us as He sees fit for our private investments in His presence.

During the Video

The Value of Private Worship

- Who in Scripture do we see practicing private worship? In these examples, what is involved in seeking God's presence in secret?

  A number of examples in Scripture are noted in this lesson, including Joshua, David, Daniel, the Apostle Peter, Cornelius, and Jesus Himself. In these examples, we see the study of Scripture, meditation on God's Word, and prayer as part of private worship and seeking after God's presence.

- Why do Christians seek to pull away and have time alone with God? What is accomplished during this time?

  In Scripture, God gives many instructions for His people to meditate on His Word and to draw near to Him in prayer. Christians long to be with God, to dwell with Him, to be made more like Him, and to enjoy His presence. We are created to be worshipers, and our love for God drives us to seek Him. Private worship gives us the opportunity to develop our relationship with God through His Word and prayer.

Practical Ways to Invest in Private Worship

- What practical steps can you take to establish a habit of private worship? What should that time include?

Like corporate worship and family worship, the practice of private worship involves a focus on God's Word and prayer, but in this case, you are alone with God and focused on abiding in His presence without the distraction of other people. It's wise to follow Jesus' recommendation to go to a "closet" or quiet space where you can quietly read and pray. Select a portion of Scripture (possibly with a reading plan or through studying a book of the Bible with a commentary) and invest in prayer (possibly the prayers of the Bible as you learn to pray). Seek to be faithful, so that your communion with God is not neglected.

- If you experience dryness in private worship, what can you do to seek refreshment and renewal?

  If we face a dry season in private worship, we should continue to take time to be in God's presence, tell the Lord about the dryness, and aim to focus on God's Word. Rev. Helopoulos recommended selecting a Scripture passage about Christ and meditating on it with determination until it stirs the affections for Christ. We need to memorize the Word, meditate on the Word, and then imitate the Word. Like savoring a piece of chocolate, we ponder the Word and consider it and welcome its effect on our lives.

After the Video

- What is private worship? What do we gain by spending this time with God?

  The call to private worship is a call to act out our affections for Christ and to form a habit of coming into God's presence daily and seeking Him in His Word and prayer. Time spent in God's presence brings rewards that could include a sense of peace with God, joy in His presence, or wisdom for the day through His Word and prayer. Beyond these gifts, there is a cumulative reward of knowing God more deeply over time as we walk daily with the Lord, learn more and more from His Word, and are continually shaped into the likeness of Jesus. Truly, moments spent with God reap benefits that last a lifetime. We do not always know clearly what God is doing, but we know that He is at work to draw us near to Him and to knit our hearts with His.

- Recalling the story of Jesus' interaction with Mary and Martha, what had Martha done? Why did Jesus commend Mary's choice? What does this story teach us?

  Martha was busy preparing a meal for Jesus and His followers, and she became frustrated with her sister for not helping with the work. Instead, Mary had chosen to sit and listen to Jesus. Jesus said: "Martha, Martha, you are anxious and troubled about many things, but one thing is necessary. Mary has chosen the good portion, which will not be taken away from her" (Luke 10:41–42). Mary's love for Jesus brought her to seek His presence—not primarily to serve Him in practical ways, but to be with Him and to hear His words. We should also seek this relational depth with the Lord by investing time in His presence in private worship.

We must be careful about being so busy with kingdom work that we fail to spend time with the King Himself.

- What does your practice of private worship look like?

  This question is personal in nature and is geared to prompt you to reflect on your own practice of private worship. This is an area of our lives that we often think can be done better, and while this question is not intending to guilt you about the time that you spend with God, it is intended to make you reflect on this time as an important dimension of the Christian life.

REVIEW QUIZ

1. **D.**
   Joshua 1:8: "This Book of the Law shall not depart from your mouth, but you shall meditate on it day and night." Though these words are specifically directed to Joshua, it was also an expectation for kings of Israel such as David. Psalm 1 teaches us that "blessed is the man who . . . delight[s] in the law of the Lord, and on his law he meditates day and night" (vv. 1–2).

2. **B.**
   Mark 1:35 tells us that this was a practice of the Son of God, who desired communion with His Father: "And rising very early in the morning, while it was still dark, he departed and went out to a desolate place, and there he prayed." This ought also to be our desire.

3. **B.**
   Though it may be our longing, we need not expect instantaneous perfection in the Christian life. We ought to expect progress and not perfection. One of the ways that we can be progressively conformed to God's image and likeness is by communing with Him in private worship.

4. **D.**
   All three of these concepts were used to give perspective on the time and patience required for walking with God and reaping the benefits of private worship.

5. **C.**
   The African proverb mentioned in this lesson was "Brother, the grass grows on your path." It is used to point out that someone has been neglecting private worship. The idea is that instead of a well-worn path to the Lord, it is becoming overgrown and seldom traveled.

6. **C.**
   Rev. Helopoulos compared the spheres of worship to a three-legged stool, in which the spheres of worship support and inform one another, helping us to live all of life more fully to God's glory. A life without one of these legs of worship is not as stable as it could be.

11

Resurrected unto Worship

INTRODUCTION

This earthly life will come to an end. When that time comes, what awaits us? Scripture reveals that the experience of life in heaven will be flooded with worship. We are created for worship, in Christ we are re-created unto worship, and in the end, through Christ we will be resurrected unto worship. In this lesson, Rev. Helopoulos highlights the difference between faith in this life and sight in the next and celebrates the abundance of glory that awaits us in heaven.

LEARNING GOALS

When you have finished this lesson, you should be able to:

- Reflect on the wonder of the glory and the ever-increasing joy that awaits believers in heaven
- Explain how faith in this life and sight in the next correlate
- Discuss how God sees Himself in relation to man, the pattern of God's dwelling among His people, and how He will dwell with us in heaven

KEY IDEAS

- The communion with God that Adam and Eve lost in the fall will be surpassed in heaven when God dwells fully with His people.
- In heaven the sight of Christ will bring blessing upon blessing, happiness upon happiness to His people, and our response will be worship.
- Heaven will bring the eternal fulfillment of God's purpose in creating us to live lives of worship and fulfill His promise to re-create us for worship in Christ.

REFLECTION & DISCUSSION QUESTIONS

Before the Video

What Do You Think?

Take a moment to answer the following questions. They will prepare you for the lecture.

- How might taking time to think about heaven shape the life of the Christian? How might it affect our personal lives, our relationships, and our ministry to others?

- What will be our great focal point of heaven? What will you feel like in heaven? Even now, what are your emotions when you consider your heavenly home?

Scripture Reading

One thing have I asked of the Lord, that will I seek after: that I may dwell in the house of the Lord all the days of my life, to gaze upon the beauty of the Lord and to inquire in his temple.

—Psalm 27:4

- Why do you think dwelling in the house of the Lord is the psalmist's sole request?

During the Video

Answer the following questions while you watch the video. They will guide you through the lecture.

Heaven: Beholding Christ *0:00–13:57*

- What was unusual about Richard Baxter's ministry in Kidderminster, England? What was a key to this fruitfulness?

- In Scripture, in what ways does God convey the concept of His dwelling with His people?

Worshipers at Home in Heaven *13:57–23:31*

- What will generate all the worship in heaven?

- In Revelation 5, the supreme victory of Christ is recognized and celebrated. How is the response described? Who is engaged in worship there?

After the Video

Answer the following questions after you have finished the lecture. They will help you identify and summarize the major points.

- How will seeing God affect us? How does Scripture describe the difference between how we see things now and how we will see them in heaven? How has this beatific vision been understood historically?

  If you are in a group, have the members read 1 John 3:1–3. Ask: How ought your anticipation of seeing God manifest itself in your life now?

- When Jesus engaged the Sadducees about their disbelief in the resurrection, what proof did He give for the resurrection? How does Jesus' interaction with this concept inform our view of heaven?

  If you are in a group, invite the members to share observations about God's promise to provide an eternal home for His people. Ask: How does this promise affect your decisions in this life? Does Jesus' expression of confidence in God's faithfulness boost your own?

- In John Bunyan's allegory *The Pilgrim's Progress*, there is great joy when Christian reaches the Celestial City. How does that story reflect what we anticipate upon our arrival in heaven?

  If you are in a group, ask the members to discuss the end of a long journey and the emotions and experience of coming home. Ask: How does that process shed light on your heavenly homegoing? Invite group members to share about loved ones who they expect are now experiencing this fullness in God's presence in heaven.

PRAYER

Commit what you have learned from God's Word in this lesson to prayer.

- Praise God for His faithfulness to fulfill our calling as worshipers by providing for us in Christ to be restored to fellowship and eternal worship in heaven.
- Confess to God any ways in which you have neglected the vision of heaven and any doubts you have concerning heaven and the fullness of joy that He has promised there.

- Thank God for the promised gift of beholding the glory of Christ and worshiping Him for eternity.
- Ask God for grace to run the race of your life with endurance, looking to the joys of heaven, and investing faithfully in corporate worship, family worship, and private worship.

REVIEW QUIZ

Use these multiple-choice questions to measure what you learned from this lesson.

1. What was identified as the key to Richard Baxter's fruitful ministry?
   a. A revival of engaging in family worship
   b. Commencing ministry in a sinful city
   c. A daily practice of meditating on heaven
   d. Spending thirty minutes each day in prayer
2. What was lost in the garden of Eden that God's promise of covenant grace would restore?
   a. A place to call home
   b. The hiding place in safety
   c. Intimate communion and union with God
   d. Space to sustain and nurture life
3. In Revelation 21, how is "the holy city, new Jerusalem" described?
   a. Descending out of heaven from God
   b. Prepared as a bride adorned for her husband
   c. The dwelling place of God
   d. All of the above
4. On the Mount of Transfiguration, what motivated Peter's suggestion to set up tents?
   a. The captivating nature of the glory of the Lord
   b. The wisdom of Elijah and Moses
   c. The quiet away from the crowds
   d. The mountaintop view of the valley
5. In heaven, beholding the glory of the Lord will be something that satisfies in every way, and yet it will increase for all eternity because He is infinite.
   a. True
   b. False
6. How did Thomas Watson describe the glory of seeing Christ in heaven?
   a. "There will be joy and outstretched arms."
   b. "All lights are but eclipses compared with this glorious vision."
   c. "There is unhindered, uninterrupted, complete communion and union with God."
   d. "Blessing upon blessing upon blessing."

Answer Key—Resurrected unto Worship

REFLECTION & DISCUSSION QUESTIONS

Before the Video

What Do You Think?

These are personal questions. The answers should be based on your own knowledge and experience.

Scripture Reading

- Why do you think dwelling in the house of the Lord is the psalmist's sole request?

  The psalmist's one request is to dwell in the house of the Lord all the days of his life. He wants to gaze on the beauty of the Lord and to meditate in the temple. This prayer expresses the psalmist's understanding that God alone will satisfy his heart and that in God all perfection abides. He longs to continually seek more and more of God, for there he will find his greatest fulfillment.

During the Video

Heaven: Beholding Christ

- What was unusual about Richard Baxter's ministry in Kidderminster, England? What was a key to this fruitfulness?

  Transformation took place through Baxter's ministry among the people in Kidderminster. The city went from being notorious for sin to a place where for two generations after Baxter's death, you could walk the streets in the evening and hear the sounds of family worship being held in the homes. It is known that Baxter spent thirty minutes each day meditating on heaven, and this discipline may have been the key to his fruitful ministry. Baxter kept the reality of his eternal home in view on a daily basis, and it shaped him and his influence on others.

- In Scripture, in what ways does God convey the concept of His dwelling with His people?

  Again and again in Scripture, we see God connecting with and making His home among His people. God met with Adam and Eve in the garden of Eden. He directed Moses to build a tabernacle to represent His presence among the people of Israel. Later, the temple served this purpose. When Jesus was born, He was known as "Immanuel," which means "God with us." Jesus sends His Holy Spirit to dwell in His followers, and their bodies are a "temple" of the Holy Spirit. Heaven is proclaimed to be the place where God dwells among His people.

Worshipers at Home in Heaven

- What will generate all the worship in heaven?

  God's glory in heaven will be more incredible than anything we can imagine. The sight of the glory of God will so affect us that it will set in motion an eternal, perpetual expression of worship. We will ever be in awe as we take in more of God's glory, understand Him more fully, and love Him more deeply. The response of worship will be automatic and overflowing.

- In Revelation 5, the supreme victory of Christ is recognized and celebrated. How is the response described? Who is engaged in worship there?

  In Revelation 5, the victory of the Lamb brings an end to John's weeping and prompts the living creatures and elders around God's throne to fall down in worship. They sing a new song of worship and extol the worthiness of the Lamb. Then the angels declare the worthiness of the Lamb, followed by every creature in heaven and on earth giving praise and honor to the Lamb.

After the Video

- How will seeing God affect us? How does Scripture describe the difference between how we see things now and how we will see them in heaven? How has this beatific vision been understood historically?

  Beholding the beauty of God's glory in heaven will completely fill our hearts with joy, happiness, love, and blessing. We will be filled with awe and wonder and joy in beholding God's manifold goodness and grace. First Corinthians 13 draws this comparison: "Now we see in a mirror dimly, but then face to face. Now I know in part; then I shall know fully, even as I have been fully known" (v. 12). The reflection of a person in the mirror is flat and out of reach, nothing like the reality of the person face-to-face. In a sense, seeing God is to know Him, and this is why many theologians before John Owen understood the beatific vision as an intellectual apprehension of God as He truly is. Owen believed that we would indeed have this intellectual understanding, but he also did justice to the reality that we will see—with our eyes—the glory of God in Christ in our resurrection bodies. According to Owen, just as faith makes us partakers of grace and holiness in this life, so sight will make us partakers of blessing upon blessing.

- When Jesus engaged the Sadducees about their disbelief in the resurrection, what proof did He give for the resurrection? How does Jesus' interaction with this concept inform our view of heaven?

  Jesus spoke of God's reference to Abraham, Isaac, and Jacob in the present tense, which implies that these men are living and not dead. Jesus spoke of them as if God is still in covenant relationship with them, which indeed He is. This interaction boosts our faith in the resurrection and demonstrates how our covenant relationship with God continues into eternity—we will one day be at home with

Him forever. God is fulfilling His promises to Abraham, Isaac, and Jacob even now, and He will continue to do so forever.

- In John Bunyan's allegory *The Pilgrim's Progress*, there is great joy when Christian reaches the Celestial City. How does that story reflect what we anticipate upon our arrival in heaven?

  In The Pilgrim's Progress, *Christian left his home to travel to the Celestial City. He endured a difficult journey with little comfort along the way. It was a relief to reach the safety of his destination, and a delight to see his faith turned to sight. At last, as he arrived, Christian knew the certainty of the things he had believed, and he could walk in the presence of God and experience the deep satisfaction of his soul. So it will be with our arrival in heaven; we will have our faith turned to sight and know the certainty of what and of whom we have believed. To reach our eternal resting place and to experience the satisfaction of seeing God and knowing Him face-to-face will bring a joy beyond our expectations.*

REVIEW QUIZ

1. **C.**
   Richard Baxter spent thirty minutes a day meditating on heaven as a source for the fruitfulness of his ministry and the transformation that was experienced at Kidderminster. Not only did this shape Baxter's life, but it also shaped his ministry and thus the lives of others.

2. **C.**
   Adam and Eve lost intimate communion with God, but the promise of the coming Redeemer foreshadowed the restoration of this relationship and God's intention to dwell with His people intimately once again.

3. **D.**
   All these references are used for heaven in Revelation 21:2–3: "And I saw the holy city, new Jerusalem, coming down out of heaven from God, prepared as a bride adorned for her husband. And I heard a loud voice from the throne saying, 'Behold, the dwelling place of God is with man. He will dwell with them, and they will be his people, and God himself will be with them as their God.'"

4. **A.**
   Peter was captivated by the glory of the Lord and wanted to dwell in that glory forever. The full glory of who Jesus is was seen on that day, as we will see Him when He returns.

5. **A.**
   As hard as it is to imagine something being completely satisfying and yet becoming even more satisfying, Rev. Helopoulos said, "Beholding the glory of the Lord will be something that satisfies in every way, and yet it will increase for all of eternity because He is infinite."

6. **B.**

Thomas Watson said of the beauty of heaven: "There will be glory beyond hyperbole. If the sun were ten thousand times brighter than it is, it could not so much as shadow out this glory. In the heavenly horizon we shall behold beauty in its first magnitude and highest elevation there. We shall see the King in His glory. All lights are but eclipses compared with this glorious vision."

Benefits of the Fear of God

INTRODUCTION

The fear of God both express the state of a person's [illegible] experience the fear of God, they begin taking [illegible]